PRAISE FOR
FIGHTING DIRTY

"*Fighting Dirty* is a compelling page-turner and a tribute to all those people who have dedicated their lives to working together to protect their community against seemingly insurmountable big government and big corporate forces."

JOHN JACKSON
Citizen activist and co-author of *Chemical Nightmare:
The Unnecessary Legacy of Toxic Waste*

"*Fighting Dirty* is a story that amplifies the voices, strength, and resilience of a rural and Indigenous community that fought to protect the local environment from the contaminant risks of garbage. It's also an important resource that challenges public health and municipal officials to ensure stronger evidence-based decisions. This is a must-read for other communities facing the same flawed and outdated regulatory processes that enable the Goliaths rather than the Davids to win."

ANNE EHRLICH
Concerned Citizens of Brant, professor emerita, McMaster University

"In *Fighting Dirty* Poh-Gek Forkert recounts a story that is all too often told around the globe of a community facing grave environmental threats. Most of us pay very little attention to stories like these, assuming that it will never happen to us. Until it does. Then we are forced to realize that the institutions and agencies we assume will protect us can't always be counted on. It is local champions with their passion to protect their families, homes, and communities who are the ones who really make a difference. This is a story of such champions and their decades-long fight to protect their community."

GRAHAM FLINT
President, Gravel Watch Ontario

"*Fighting Dirty* is an inspiring tribute to a small rural community and a nearby First Nations community who combined forces to fight the world's largest waste disposal company and its enablers in the Ministry of the Environment. Poh-Gek Forkert is a talented storyteller with a compelling David and Goliath story to tell."

JOHN SWAIGEN
Counsel, Ecojustice; author of *How to Fight for What's Right:*
The Citizen's Guide to Public Interest Law

"*Fighting Dirty* tells the astonishing tale of one community's battle against a deep-pocketed waste company. The Richmond Landfill leaks contaminants into groundwater, which migrates onto neighbouring farmlands and into domestic wells, leaving families unable to drink their well water and unable to collect rainwater because of the guano from flocks of seagulls flying overhead. Forkert's moving portrayal of the community's courage and determination shows that citizens working together can respond to the incapacity of the very government ministries and agencies that they trust to protect them, and can mobilize allies to effectively fight environmental threats to their community. Best of all, in this case the good citizens win."

BRYAN SMITH
Chair, Oxford Coalition for Social Justice

FIGHTING DIRTY

HOW A SMALL COMMUNITY TOOK ON BIG TRASH

POH-GEK FORKERT

Between the Lines
Toronto

Fighting Dirty:
How a Small Community
Took on Big Trash
© 2017 Poh-Gek Forkert

First published in 2017
by Between the Lines
401 Richmond Street West, Studio 277
Toronto, Ontario M5V 3A8 Canada
1-800-718-7201
www.btlbooks.com

TD789.C32N37 2017
363.72'80971359
C2017-903050-7
C2017-903051-5

Cover and text design by Clea Forkert
Printed in Canada

Typefaces: Perpetua Titling, Portrait
and Venus Halbfett

MIX
Paper from
responsible sources
FSC® C103567
www.fsc.org

We acknowledge for their financial support
of our publishing activities: the Government
of Canada; the Canada Council for the
Arts, which last year invested $153 million
to bring the arts to Canadians throughout
the country; and the Government of
Ontario through the Ontario Arts Council,
the Ontario Book Publishers Tax
Credit program, and the Ontario Media
Development Corporation.

**Library and Archives Canada
Cataloguing in Publication**
Forkert, Poh-Gek, author
Fighting dirty : how a small community
took on big trash / Poh-Gek Forkert.
Includes index.
Issued in print and electronic formats.
ISBN 978-1-77113-324-1 (softcover).--
ISBN 978-1-77113-325-8 (EPUB).--
ISBN 978-1-77113-326-5 (PDF)

1. Refuse and refuse disposal—
Social aspects—Ontario—Napanee.
2. Fills (Earthwork—Environmental
aspects—Ontario—Napanee.
3. Pollution prevention—Ontario—
Napanee—Citizen participation.
I. Title.

Canada Council
for the Arts

Conseil des Arts
du Canada

Canadä

ONTARIO ARTS COUNCIL
CONSEIL DES ARTS DE L'ONTARIO
an Ontario government agency
un organisme du gouvernement de l'Ontario

To Lutz, Kirsten, and Clea

CONTENTS

PREFACE

A colleague who knew of my work as a toxicologist suggested I accompany her to a gathering of citizens trying to stop a mega-dump near their small town in southeastern Ontario. "Come," she said. "I think you'll find it interesting." That meeting in the summer of 2005 triggered a sequence of events that would change my life. For the next ten years, I became embroiled—both as active participant and then as chronicler/historian—in a fight between a small but determined group of rural folks and the biggest garbage company in the world.

The fight had already been underway for half a dozen years, but now the opposition was ramping up. Terrible things can happen to a community's land, air, and water when a little dump becomes a mega-dump. As the pile of soil-covered garbage rose ever higher, these folks had already been rocked by some hard truths about rancid air, rat infestations, and tainted wells.

When I walked into that Tyendinaga Township community hall, all eyes turned towards me. First of all, I was clearly an outsider. I am Malaysian by birth, and the rural population of southeastern Ontario is overwhelmingly white. Second, I was a research scientist, then still teaching at Queen's University, and very much an urban person. These were rural people, whether local for generations or transplants from the city—the kind who mark the country custom of pulling over to the side of the road when a funeral procession drives past. Of those born and bred here, many of their ancestors had come when potato crops failed in Ireland in the 1840s, and many still planted potatoes in their family-owned, rock-strewn holdings.

It struck me early on, though, that for all their deep roots in this land, they didn't have a voice in decisions about how that land was to be used—or, in this case, abused. After that first meeting, I got hooked. I started taking notes, attended more meetings, went to the land registry and the catacombs of the local weekly newspaper, appeared as a witness at a public hearing, and interviewed all the major players on the anti-dump side. As a scientist, I was trained to be dispassionate, objective, logical, rational—and none of that changed. But for the first time in my personal life, I joined forces with a community of people as they fought to avert environmental catastrophe.

This is a story of how a small group of activists and a First Nation community, the Mohawks of the Bay of Quinte (MBQ), fought the world's largest garbage company, first over a landfill expansion and then over the dump's terms of closure and environmental monitoring. I wanted both to tell this remarkable story of "fighting dirty" from the citizens' vantage and to offer practical lessons to others facing unwanted, environmentally harmful development.

A group of dedicated people, working in tandem, can indeed topple a giant. But know, too, that it is difficult and that the cost—in time, effort, and money—is unimaginable. Like a soldier in combat, I got close to the men and women in the trenches. Their struggles and suffering moved me deeply, and revisiting their hardship to write this book was just as wrenching as hearing it for the first time.

ACKNOWLEDGEMENTS

Fighting Dirty owes much to contributions from participants in the landfill fight. This is almost certainly an incomplete list: Mike Bossio, Ian Munro, Marilyn Kendall, Margaret Walsh, the late Steve Geneja, Janelle Tulloch, Bernice Thompson, Steve Medd, Ed File, the late Howard O'Connor, Jeff Whan, Fred Whalen, Kelley Hineman, Carolyn Butts, Wayne Chadwick, and Marilyn Carey—thanks indeed to each one. I am greatly indebted to the late Allan Gardiner for early stories of the dump fight and for generously contributing time to answer all my queries; and to the late Mary Lynne Sammon for her passionate commitment to this fight. Thanks to Trish Rae for education and assistance with Mohawk history; to Kevin Shipley for assistance with geology and other landfill issues; to Wilf Ruland for information on hydrogeology; to archivists Jane Foster and Shelley Respondek (Lennox and Addington Museum and Archives), Sharon White (Hastings County Historical Society), and Amanda Hill (Community Archives of Belleville and Hastings County) for facilitating access to historical data and archival photographs; to Ben and Janet Sutcliffe, Betty and Doug Cranston, and Rick Shelley for their stories; to Seth DuChene for assistance and access to archives of the *Napanee Beaver*; to Chief R. Donald Maracle for information and conversations about the Mohawk community and the landfill fight; and to Richard Lindgren for the opportunity of working with him on the Richmond Landfill case and for guidance and advice throughout. To Lawrence Scanlan, who took my massive "scientific" manuscript and highlighted the storylines of people for people—thank you. Many thanks to Jan Walter and Jamie Swift, who reviewed and guided me through the process of getting this book to press. My gratitude also to early readers Jeff Whan, Wilf Ruland, Marilyn Kendall, Rick Lindgren, and Ian Munro. And finally, special thanks to my husband, Lutz, for photography and to my daughter Clea for designing this book.

FORMER RICHMOND TOWNSHIP
(NOW PART OF TOWN OF GREATER NAPANEE)

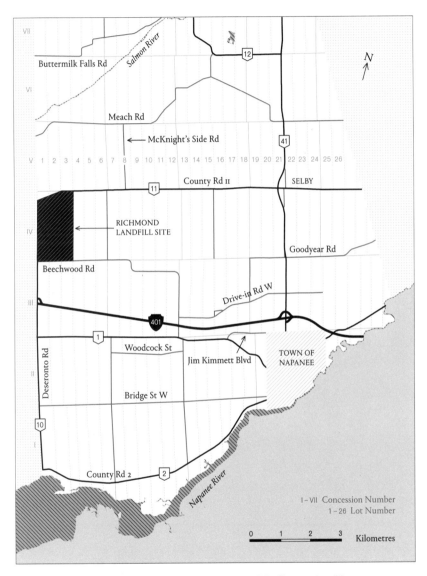

Richmond Landfill Site: Lots 1, 2 and 3, Concession IV
Map courtesy of County of Lennox and Addington

CHAPTER 1

FROM THE LAB TO THE TRENCHES

"Where is the Ministry of Environment?" I asked.
They all laughed.

After attending my first anti-dump meeting in the Tyendinaga Township community hall in 2005, I was contacted by Richard Lindgren, a staff member of the Canadian Environmental Law Association (CELA) and the lawyer for the Concerned Citizens Committee of Tyendinaga and Environs (CCCTE). He was looking for a toxicologist who could carry out health risk assessments relating to the landfill near Napanee, and asked if I was interested in taking it on. Having investigated chemicals throughout my scientific career, I felt well prepared for the assignment. I was also intrigued by the twists and turns of the story, as Rick explained them to me.

A waste management company had initiated plans for a massive expansion of what had been a small, local dump, the Richmond Landfill. The first regulatory requirement was to prepare terms of reference of the environmental assessment (EA).[1] This document, submitted in June 1999, described the scope of the proposed project. The provincial minister of the environment had approved the terms of reference for the proposed expansion. That decision headed for the courts, and after four years of legal wrangling, the dump expansion plan landed back on the table in late 2004.

Given my interest in dumps and the risks they pose, I agreed to work as a toxicology consultant for the project's opponents and their lawyer. My interest in the topic goes back several decades. Soon after I had come to Queen's University in 1982 as a professor and scientist, I had established a team to research toxic chemicals, primarily focused on the disposition and metabolism of chemical contaminants when they gain entry to a biological system, including the human body. The chemicals we investigated included those present in groundwater, air, and food. We found, as did other scientists, that when exposure to certain chemicals occurred, some of these chemicals were transformed and became more toxic and/or more carcinogenic than the parent compounds. In other words, chemical exposure elevated risk. We published our findings in scientific journals, presented at scientific meetings, and spoke at other universities and regulatory agencies including Health Canada, Environment Canada, and the U.S. Environmental Protection Agency.

In 2001, CBC TV's *Marketplace* had featured our research team and a rural couple near Ottawa whose drinking water was contaminated with trichloroethylene. We were studying that chemical, which is used as an industrial solvent and is a common environmental contaminant, including in groundwater. Constituents of waste are carried from landfills in a solution of existing liquids, rainwater, and snowmelt called leachate. In this case, leachate, containing contaminants from an old municipal dump, had tainted the groundwater supplying the couple's wells, and they were being told they couldn't drink their water. The mother had been pregnant when they moved into the area. She drank the well water, bathed her daughter in it, and used it to mix formula for her newborn son. She was greatly concerned about making her children sick, if not now, then in days to come.

The *Marketplace* episode marked my team's first direct exposure to the effects of dumps. It also brought us requests for commentary and expert testimony for court cases involving trichloroethylene and other chemicals. In the course of this work, which included carrying out health risk assessments, I discovered that many communities in Canada are plagued by contamination with chemical toxicants.

As I was joining the Richmond Landfill fight, the terms of reference had already been approved by the minister of the environment, and the next step in the legislative process—the environmental assessment—was in progress. My first step was to meet with landfill opponents and better acquaint myself with the issues. It was at the end of September 2005, in the home of Ben Sutcliffe, just across the road from the dumpsite, that I first met four of the key players: Allan Gardiner, Janelle Tulloch, Mike Bossio, and Margaret Walsh. They told me about the impact of the dump on their day-to-day lives. I could hardly believe the extent to which their quality of life had been compromised. "Where is the Ministry of Environment?" I asked. They all laughed.

***

In November 2005, Waste Management of Canada Corporation (WMC) submitted documentation for its environmental assessment for the proposed expansion of the Richmond Landfill site, and the public comment period began. Richard Lindgren requested that I review the assessment's public health components. Dump opponents were upset and angry that the public comment period was scheduled over the Christmas holidays. They asked the Ontario Ministry of the Environment (MOE) to grant them an extension, a request the ministry denied. I was not pleased either, and I ended up spending that Christmas beside a wood stove with a computer on my lap.

My overall conclusion was that the environmental assessment and its supporting documents provided insufficient evidence to demonstrate that the landfill and its proposed expansion posed no health risks to area residents. My comments, along with those from other expert consultants, were sent to the Ministry of the Environment. Despite the timing, I was surprised to find out later how many citizens had responded during the public comment period.

The ministry received over six thousand public comments regarding the environmental assessment. Waste Management requested a two-month extension for rebuttal. The ministry granted their request. Dump opponents were furious when they found out about the extension. "It's simply not fair," wrote Marilyn Kendall in a "Discourse on the Dump" column in the *Napanee Beaver*.[2]

Over time I got to know more people in the citizens' group, and I also met and worked with Chief Don Maracle, who was in the fight for his people, the Mohawks of the Bay of Quinte, on the nearby Tyendinaga Mohawk Territory. I was struck by how dedicated these folks were, despite their low odds of winning this fight. They were too terrified to think much about the final outcome—but it was clear in their minds what they were fighting for.

The words "clean air" and "clean water" have greater meaning for me now. The great fear of those who live in the landfill's long shadow is contamination of their wells—the source of drinking water for their families and livestock. They know that contaminated water is impossible to remediate for human and animal consumption. And they had no confidence in the Ministry of the Environment, which was responsible for oversight of the landfill, to protect them. Anxieties about the air they breathe and the water they drink have compromised their sense of wellbeing, and, in some cases, their health. This experience underscored for me the extent to which environmental health and human health are linked—and how human health must include that sense of wellbeing. That has been taken away from them. Local farmer Allan Gardiner called it "paradise lost."

Once the concerned citizens won the battle to stop the dump expansion, they would have to fight to have the site closed safely. It cost them eight years of their lives to stop the expansion and another five years for closure—and it's still not over. But still, a small band of environmentalists has bested a multinational company. Would they do it again? Mike Bossio, a former chair of the citizens' committee and one of its longest-serving members, was emphatic when I put that question to him. He would, he said, "because it was the right thing to do and because they did the wrong thing."

As an expert consultant, I provided technical and scientific information. I went to the dump meetings and kept in touch, recording the events that embroiled the committee—sometimes as a scientist, sometimes as a historian. But it was these foot soldiers on the front lines who demonstrated to me what it really means to be caretakers of our environment and our earth.

CHAPTER 2

DAVID VS. GOLIATH

*As the public consultation process developed,
so did opposition from local citizens.*

Lawyer Richard Lindgren calls the Richmond Landfill battle the longest environmental struggle he has encountered and one that has involved every aspect of environmental law. In it, you will meet a Mohawk chief, and a dedicated group of activists and their lawyer, recalling the many twists and turns of a dump fight that took place over two decades. Here, to get us started, is a brief summary of some major signposts along the way.

It all began in 1954 when Fred Sutcliffe Sr., an English immigrant farmer, arrived in Richmond Township in southeastern Ontario. When he started collecting garbage in the community, that was the beginning of the local dumpsite. The years passed, and the pile of garbage grew. In 1985, Sutcliffe applied for an expansion of his dumpsite, gaining approval from the Ministry of the Environment to receive garbage from all municipalities of Ontario. He promptly sold the dumpsite to Tricil Ltd., a waste management company, and Sutcliffe's dumpsite became the Richmond Landfill.

After the sale to Tricil, angry residents gathered at a meeting. Winnifred Jackson, an elderly resident whose family had purchased their farm in 1900, expressed the community's sense of betrayal to Sutcliffe, after having welcomed him to their community and their homes. This was the beginning of an opposition campaign led by Allan Gardiner, but the farmer and his community soon realized how powerless they actually were.

Richmond Landfill passed on from Tricil Ltd. to Laidlaw Waste Systems Ltd., which over the intervening years changed its name to Canadian Waste Services Ltd., then to Canadian Waste Services Inc., and finally to Waste Management of Canada Corporation. In 1998, Canadian Waste Services announced plans for a landfill expansion to make space for dumping millions of tonnes of garbage. As required, they carried out public consultations on the terms of reference that had to be submitted for the proposed expansion. As the public consultation process developed, so did opposition from local citizens.

Before the consultations were over, Margaret Walsh—a diminutive woman who was then reeve of Tyendinaga Township—had emerged as an unlikely activist. She called the first dump protest meeting, and invited the Mohawks from the nearby reserve. At this meeting, a Mohawk Elder collapsed and died after giving a rousing speech. Mike Bossio, who would play a key role in the dump fight, was there beside Margaret when the tragedy happened.

The landfill company forged ahead with its expansion plans, and in June 1999, Canadian Waste Services submitted terms of reference for its proposal to the Ministry of the Environment. In July, the citizens (now calling themselves Concerned Citizens Committee of Tyendinaga and Environs) retained environmental lawyer Richard Lindgren. Enter also Chief Don Maracle of the Mohawks of the Bay of Quinte, who would become a formidable leader in the dump fight. Now the battle lines were drawn.

In September 1999, the minister of the environment approved the terms of reference. The issue headed to the courts and was tied up there for four years. At the end of the legal wrangling, the proposed expansion was back on the table and public consultations ramped up. During this period, new activists entered the picture—Steve Medd, Ian Munro, Marilyn Kendall, and Jeff Whan, a well-educated bunch. Geologist Steve Medd, for example, took on the role of educating the public on the characteristics of the Richmond Landfill site—fractured limestone is a risky place to store garbage.

In November 2005, Waste Management of Canada Corporation submitted documentation for the environmental assessment for the proposed expansion. Thousands of letters, an unprecedented number, flooded into the Ministry of the Environment opposing the project. A year later, the minister announced the decision to reject Waste Management's proposal for safety reasons. A key issue was that the geology of the site was unsuitable and unsafe.

And then the activists turned their fight to the closure of the Richmond Landfill. This dragged on for years before the landfill closed down in June 2011. But it still wasn't over. In January 2012, the Ministry of the Environment's director issued a document with conditions outlining the terms of closure of the landfill. Without delay, CCCTE applied for leave to appeal seven of the document's conditions. While this was going on, the environment minister approved terms of reference for a *new* proposed landfill expansion called the Beechwood Road Environmental Centre (BREC) at a site right next to the old one. Dump opponents were aghast.

In March 2012, the Environmental Review Tribunal (ERT) granted leave to CCCTE to appeal all seven conditions in the director's document. Mediation between the parties (CCCTE, Mohawks of the Bay of Quinte, the ministry, Waste Management, and a local citizens' group called Napanee Green Lights) resulted in agreement on three of the conditions. But the other four were to be resolved at a tribunal public hearing.

The tribunal hearing began in Belleville in April 2015 and continued until that June. One indisputable fact emerged—leachate had migrated out of the boundaries of the Richmond Landfill site and contaminated domestic wells and groundwater. Especially contentious was the issue of how much 1,4-dioxane, the best leachate indicator, was permitted in drinking water. This prevalent organic compound, used in everything from cosmetics to paints to pesticides, is classified as a probable human carcinogen. On behalf of the CCCTE, I advocated for the lowest possible level (1 microgram per litre), while the recommendations of the experts for the Ministry of the Environment and the proponent were much higher.

In December 2015, the tribunal released its decision—drinking water standard 1 microgram per litre—and ordered Waste Management to resolve the issues surrounding leachate contamination of groundwater, surface water, and nearby lands to that standard.

A small group of concerned citizens in rural Ontario and a group of First Nation people encountered many obstacles—some from their own government—as they fought together to protect their air and water. They bested a garbage giant that came to expand a dump that was already polluting their environment. David was pitted against Goliath, and just as in the Bible story, the much smaller opponent would ultimately prevail. As I write in 2017, it looks tentatively like the battle has been won. But to this day, the contamination issues remained unresolved. For the anti-dump activists and the Mohawks of the Bay of Quinte, the job is not done, and they can't take their eyes off the ball.

Both sides were bloodied in this contest. More than a quarter-million dollars was raised by dump opponents to pay for the expenses of this interminable battle—a staggering sum for a small, rural community. And more than eight thousand letters on the issue were written to the provincial government.

Goliath looked like this: The dump, once a small family-run operation, changed hands several times over the years but corporate owners first entered the picture in 1987. The current owner is Waste Management of Canada Corporation, a subsidiary of Waste Management Inc. based in Houston, Texas. The parent company operates close to three hundred landfills all over North America, and had sales/revenue in 2015 of almost US$13 billion.[3]

What about David? Although thousands of people in and around Napanee would get involved in some way (writing letters, baking cookies, selling raffle tickets, joining protests), the core group was made up of about a dozen people. That core would change over the course of years and decades, as members aged and passed away. Many were farmers or semi-retired farmers, but some brought a great deal of education and experience to the table—a geologist, an engineer, a software expert, a telecommunications expert, a teacher, an editor, a Mohawk chief with political smarts. They were a varied and creative bunch, but they formed a formidable alliance that got tighter as the years passed.

This is their story. It is one that should be told, as it may point the way for other communities facing similarly ill-conceived projects.

CHAPTER 3

THE LOCAL GARBAGEMAN

Neighbours found Fred Sutcliffe to be a quiet,
well-spoken man. When an employee was caught stealing money
from him, he merely said, "He must have needed it."

Richmond Township lies to the east and adjacent to the Tyendinaga Mohawk Territory in southeastern Ontario. The township sits on the Napanee Plain, one of North America's great limestone plains. The bedrock here is a sheet of limestone some fifty metres thick, all underlain by the granite and gneiss of the Canadian Shield. Limestone is one of the most soluble of the common types of bedrock, and long before the Ice Age, dissolution by surface water and groundwater made the limestone irregular. The stone is riddled with open fissures, sinkholes, and subterranean channels. The fractures are commonly horizontal and are connected by vertical or oblique fractures.

In recounting this story, the phrase "fractured limestone" will come up a lot. That's because a dump, and then a mega-dump, was created on a site on this limestone plain. And the question arose: Is this a good place to dump waste or not? And if not, why not?

When it comes to landfill sites, geology is key. On top of the fractured limestone bedrock is a thin layer of sediment consisting of a mixture of rocks, sand, and clay deposited by retreating glaciers. This glacial till allows surface water from rain and snowmelt to rapidly penetrate and flow readily through the fractured bedrock. Groundwater flow through this complex network of interconnected fractures is extremely variable in both direction and rate. The granite and gneiss below is less permeable than the limestone above, and the junction between them tends to be the site of a major aquifer that provides water to local wells.

Richmond Township's diverse geography includes forests, wetlands, lakes, grasslands, rivers, drumlins, and alvars. Drumlins are oval-shaped mounds of glacial till—one end is blunt and the other sloped gently—that tend to occur in groups. Lennox and Addington County has about 175 drumlins strewn across its southern end that provide good agricultural land on a limestone plain. Alvars—another unique feature of the limestone

Water emerging from fractures in limestone bedrock.
Rock cut on Deseronto Road north of the Richmond Landfill.
Photo courtesy of Lutz Forkert.

plains—are places where the limestone plain is covered by thin or no soil, resulting in sparse grassland or exposed flat rock that support a community of rare plants, birds, and animals. Farmers here have an expression that captures just how thin the soil is. "The bottom," they say, "is pretty close to the top."

Richmond is settler country—most immigrants were of Irish, English, or Scottish descent. Many were United Empire Loyalists from the United States. Others were discharged soldiers of Irish, English, and Scottish origins, and still others of German, Dutch, and French descent—all of whom were granted "free land." Later, after the potato famines of the mid-1800s, there was an influx of settlers from Ireland and Scotland. Some families in Richmond Township have been there for many generations. A saying here has it that you are a true local only if four generations of your family are buried in local graveyards. Quite a few of those families still live in the area.

It was to Richmond Township that Fred Sutcliffe Sr., a thirty-six-year-old British immigrant, tall and prematurely bald, came in the winter of 1953, looking for a farm on which to settle his family. He had been doing well as a dairy farmer in the north of England, but he left, in part, because of family disputes. As a nephew would later recount, too many family members were concentrated in the small area of Lancashire that he lived in, and he wanted to leave them behind.

Although he had been known as an easygoing fellow who generally got along well with family members, one incident particularly irked Sutcliffe.

He had told his brother of his intention to apply for a lease on a Duchy farm (property given by royal charter to the Prince of Wales as the sovereign's eldest son). The brother quietly and promptly submitted an application for the same property and was granted the lease. Fred Sutcliffe felt betrayed, to say the least—and it was one of the reasons he left the country.

***

In December 1953, Fred Sutcliffe purchased a farm in Richmond Township from John and Lillian ter Braak for ten thousand dollars: $1,400 in cash and a mortgage of $8,600, the amount remaining from the mortgage the couple took on when they had bought the property. One of the ter Braaks may have been a distant relative of Sutcliffe's wife, Mary, which was likely what brought the Sutcliffes to the area in the first place. Fred moved into the homestead with Mary and their five children: two sons, Fred Jr. and Ben, and three daughters, Mary, Sylvia, and Eileen.

Fred's original objective in the new country was to run a dairy farm. As a teenager in Britain, he showed cattle, and he was especially proud of a prize-winning bull that he rode around the farm. His new property in Canada came with a herd of cattle and a contract for milk and cream. Fred was apparently assured that the cows had been bred earlier in the fall and that there would be calves and milk in the spring. But as winter progressed and the snow piled high, he realized that there would be no calves and no milk. Although cows can be bred at any time during the year, some farmers preferred to breed them in summer or early fall so that the calves were born nine months later. This timing was an economical strategy, as the animals could then be fed on grass. In the case of Fred Sutcliffe's cows, either the breeding was unsuccessful due to an infertile bull or, more likely, the bull was sold before Sutcliffe took possession of the herd. In any case, there were no calves or milk that spring, and no short-term prospect of an income from the herd.

Sutcliffe had been a successful cattle farmer in Britain and had sold his farm prior to moving to Canada. However, at that time, strict limits were imposed on funds that could be taken out of the country, and he could not bring a substantial amount of money with him when he emigrated. He thus found himself in a precarious situation, with no immediate source of income to provide for his large family.

Although the Sutcliffe farm had some of the most productive agricultural land in the area because of a drumlin that provided deep fertile soil, agricultural farming was at least as long-term a commitment as livestock farming. On the other hand, raising cattle for beef or dairy required substantial capital investment, and neither could yield immediate benefits for Sutcliffe's family. Realizing he could not rely on earnings from farming in the short term, he came up with an alternate plan.

This followed a chance encounter with Walter Rankin, a local postman who also operated a municipal dumpsite on his farm property on River Road beside the Napanee River. At that time garbage was not collected; people took their own refuse to deposit on the site beside the banks of the river. (Environmental awareness was a concept slow to form. Those who purchased properties along the Napanee River would find that the riverbank had been used as a nineteenth-century dumping ground for wood ash, tin, glass bottles, and broken china.)

Rankin was finding his two jobs onerous. He liked delivering mail but was looking for an opportunity to shed the dumpsite. At the same time, Sutcliffe was desperately looking for an opportunity of any kind. The discussions between the two led Sutcliffe to purchase from Rankin a municipal contract and a truck for hauling garbage. Sutcliffe then set up his own company—Sutcliffe Sanitation Services Ltd.—to collect garbage from residences in the area. Many residents were pleased to have the service. Now they could put their garbage outside their homes, and Sutcliffe Sanitation would take it away.

As of 1954, Sutcliffe trucked the garbage he collected to a site on his own farm property on Lot 2, dumping it over an embankment just east and north of the original barn. The garbage was burned each night up until 1974, when that practice was no longer permitted because of its environmental impact. However, Sutcliffe continued to dump garbage behind his barn. When provincial licensing became mandatory, Sutcliffe Sanitation applied for and was granted Provisional Certificate of Approval No. 371203, issued in February 1971, for disposal of domestic, commercial, and non-hazardous solid industrial waste, at an annual rate of 15,000 tonnes in an area of 3.6 hectares (9.0 acres). Sutcliffe renewed the licence as needed, and in the course of time the approved service area was expanded to encompass nine municipalities in the three counties of Lennox and Addington, Prince Edward, and Hastings.

In the meantime, the Sutcliffe family was adjusting to their new home in Richmond and to Fred's enterprise. As the children grew up, they contributed to what essentially became a family operation. Sons and daughters helped in the daily collection of garbage.

As for Sutcliffe, he worked hard at his new role as local garbageman, and was soon raising a herd of purebred cattle on his farm on Lot 2. Neighbours found him to be a quiet, well-spoken man, always pleasant and friendly. He was unusually non-confrontational. When an employee was caught stealing money from him, he merely said, "He must have needed it."

Fred Sutcliffe was well liked in the community, and when it came to garbage disposal, his neighbours preferred to deal with him rather than with his wife, Mary. She was described by neighbours as having a sharp tongue and was perceived as being intent on charging them more for dumping garbage. "Fred would tell people to give him a dollar to dump their garbage, whereas Mary would ask for five dollars or more," recalled a neighbour. Others were of the opinion that Mary's parsimony was justified to compensate for Fred's overly generous disposition. Such were the dynamics of life in a small rural community. However, attitudes could also bend when circumstances took a turn, and people became more sympathetic to Mary when tragedy struck the family. Sylvia, now married to Basil Young, had a son, Duane Young, in 1964. The little boy was about five years old and in the care of his grandfather, Fred Sutcliffe, when he was killed in an accident at the dumpsite. Most of the community turned out for the child's funeral and the burial at the Riverside Cemetery in Napanee.

Despite this tragic accident, the family remained optimistic about the future of the business, which had become a successful operation in the 1970s and 1980s. Sutcliffe began acquiring farmland with a long-term objective of further expanding his waste operation. His logical choices were the two farm properties adjoining his own, Lot 3 to the east and Lot 1 to the west.

In 1977, Fred Sutcliffe purchased Lot 3, the John Mowers farm of seventy acres. Kind man that he was, he told Mowers and his two daughters that they could continue to live in their home for as long as they needed to. Only after the family had moved to Napanee did he demolish the house and barn. He advised them of the demolition, explaining that the buildings were in a bad state of disrepair and falling down. John Mowers died in 1978 at the age of 92. Irene, now in her nineties, is the only surviving daughter.

Several years later Sutcliffe turned his attention to the property on Lot 1, Concession IV. In 1984, Sutcliffe purchased the Mowbray property of ninety acres for a hundred thousand dollars. Thus by the mid-1980s, in addition to the two hundred acres of the original purchase of Lot 2, the Sutcliffe family now owned land in Lots 1, 2, and 3, totalling an area of approximately 355 acres. The dumpsite was in the south half of Lot 2 and conveniently located in terms of road access: on the south side of County Road 11 (Selby Road), the east side of County Road 10 (Deseronto Road), and 1.4 kilometres north of Highway 401.

In time, the territory from which garbage was collected also increased, and the business thrived. Sutcliffe enjoyed driving his truck around collecting garbage from his neighbours. His services were appreciated, and he had a reputation for being helpful. Elderly customers, especially women, who had difficulty hauling their garbage to the roadside could leave it close to the house to be collected. The surrounding communities were generally satisfied with Sutcliffe Sanitation Services. During this time, few regulations were in place for local dumps, and the Sutcliffe operations were rather informal. However, they were generally regarded by the public as satisfactory, as garbage was picked up regularly and disposed of.

The scale of Fred Sutcliffe's operation was small compared to what it developed into later on. The waste came from local communities. No more than half a dozen trucks collected garbage. On his way home each evening, Sutcliffe would drive slowly, and if there was garbage along the route, he would stop and his sons would jump off the truck to pick up the debris. There were no garbage odours, no noisy truck traffic, no refuse along the roadsides, and no discontented neighbours. When the situation changed, it was unexpected. Sutcliffe's neighbours were even more surprised when they eventually found out that he had deceived them, an act that seemed totally out of character for the man.

CHAPTER 4

THE COOKIE MONSTER

"The company put on what they called 'kitchen table meetings'... They put out tea and coffee and cookies—but they were not *homemade! They were store bought!"*
—Margaret Walsh, former reeve of Tyendinaga Township

I went to see Margaret Walsh, the first elected official to oppose the dump expansion, in her home in February 2015. It was the middle of one of the coldest winters I have experienced since coming to Canada decades ago. She lives on a countryside road, McCullough Road, west of Napanee in a century-old clapboard place she's been in since 1952, the year she got married. It's a white, aluminum-clad farmhouse (Margaret calls the exterior siding tin) with a black roof. An old schoolhouse, now used as a storage shed, is similarly outfitted on the right as you come onto the property, with an ample red barn behind.

Margaret welcomed me into her compact dining room, with hip-high pine wainscotting all around and a wood stove blazing in the corner. Her dog and cat were eager to greet me; Margaret parked them both in the summer kitchen and brought me slippers to keep my feet warm. The dining room table, I noticed, was set out for tea—with little trays of cashews along with date squares and banana muffins, the baked goods all homemade. An hour or so later, as I got set to leave, she armed me with a ziplock bag and insisted I take a goodly number of the treats home. They were delicious; Margaret retains a reputation in the community for the quality of her muffins, tarts, cookies, and pies. No one appreciates her baking more than Chief Don Maracle—knowing this, Margaret regularly drops a plateful of cookies off at his band office.

She is a diminutive, soft-spoken woman, just five feet tall with apple cheeks and a winning smile. Margaret was born in 1923, which makes her ninety-two when I visit. The right word is no longer always there on the tip of her tongue, and that is a source of great frustration for her. On the other hand, how many people that age live alone in a farmhouse? The five-bedroom house is heated by propane supplemented by wood. "I keep the wood stove burning all day in the winter—makes me feel cozy. It is also a backup for when the power goes off," she said. Most others of a similar vintage have settled into a rocking chair in a nursing home. Margaret's husband, Bill, the former clerk-treasurer of Tyendinaga Township, died in 1986, so she has been tending this place essentially by herself for a long time. A local farmer leases the farmland to grow corn and other crops.

One of the abiding images from that visit was of Margaret tearing down the driveway to back up a big flatbed truck that had come in to drop off a load of timber. She was afraid the truck would block my car, so out she went, coatless and in boots, to instruct the driver to retreat. There was something almost girlish about the sight.

Margaret came back in, a little breathless, and explained that one of her sons comes around regularly to see how she's doing and to cut and split firewood. Still, she's the one who has to bring in the wood and feed the fire. When the men from the landfill company came around early during the dump expansion initiative trying to get people who lived close to the local dump to warm to the notion of it becoming a mega-dump, it must have been tempting for them to dismiss Margaret Walsh. She was sixty-four then—retirement age. But she was also the reeve of Tyendinaga Township, and the first elected official in the long and sometimes sorry saga of the Richmond Landfill to smell, as it were, a rat.

Margaret remembered the public consultation meetings Canadian Waste Services carried out for the dump expansion. They were about the terms of reference of the environmental assessment. She went to one they called a "kitchen table" meeting—and never went back. Held at a home of one of the residents, it was supposed to give the impression of being "cozy" and "homey," she explained, her words dripping with sarcasm. "They were sweet," she said of the company men. "But I resented them. They were so nice that I did not trust them. I thought they were up to no good for the community."

Their first cardinal sin, as Margaret saw it, was that while they had come to the meeting with refreshments and cookies, the latter were clearly purchased in a store. The newcomers hadn't done their homework. When people in the country bring friends and neighbours into their homes, they offer them sustenance—a meal, or coffee or tea, or something from their own oven. The same rule applied when someone in the community died: you showed your respect by bringing food around to the house, food of your own making. The casseroles, soups, and pies go into the freezer so the grieving family is spared the duty of cooking while feeding friends and relations who have come to the wake and funeral. Margaret summed it up for me: "Country folk are different from town and city folk."

Over the years and decades, the company men changed as the dump changed hands. Tricil morphed into Laidlaw and then into Canadian

Waste Services and then into Waste Management of Canada Corporation, as one landfill company was bought up or replaced by another, changed its name, or came under the auspices of a multinational. But one thing was constant, and it irked Margaret Walsh. The men from away never bothered to learn local customs. She took this as a sign of insincerity. The corporate types literally looked down on her, and that was a mistake.

Margaret may have looked like a little old lady, but she was made of sterner stuff. That day she sat by the dining room table and gave the bare bones of her life story, laughing often and bending over at the waist each time. Margaret was born a Kelly in Dundas County, near Cornwall on the St. Lawrence River, the oldest of three children. She went to normal school (as teachers' college was then called) in Ottawa and began teaching primary school at the age of eighteen. "It was like playing with children," she said. She retired when she was fifty-seven but soon forged a career in municipal politics, spending twenty years on local council—thirteen as reeve.

"I never lost an election," she told me. This statement was uttered with a smile but with a jolt of pride too. Margaret buckled with laughter as she recalled the incumbent reeve. She was on township council at the time, and didn't like the reeve or the way he operated. So she decided to contest him in the next election. She won. He ran against her in the next election but lost that one to Margaret again. She chuckled as she recalled that no one had dared to run against her again—she was elected by acclamation thereafter.

With a few years off to care for her kids, Margaret Walsh taught school for thirty-six years, often running a one-room schoolhouse with thirty-eight children. There were eight rows, each row a different grade—from grade one to eight. The schoolhouse would be stone cold when she arrived on a winter morning, but the older pupils were expected to get the wood stove running and to stoke it throughout the day.

Margaret's evenings were spent preparing lesson plans—"to keep one group of children busy while [she] taught another group." Her salary in the beginning was $750 a year, later raised to $900. At the same time, she was a mother of three children, and a farm wife who had to prepare meals and do the dishes and laundry, the sewing and the house cleaning. There were eighteen milking cows on the farm, among assorted other animals including pigs, chickens, and geese. Bill's father stayed with the family for fifteen years. "Grandpa used to rock the baby in the rocking chair," she recalled fondly.

Maybe she learned a thing or two about budgets and priorities, and time management and recordkeeping. In any case, Margaret was clearly trusted by voters in the township: she finally stepped down as reeve in

2010 at the age of eighty-seven. The landfill issue was still very much alive, so she remained as councillor for another four years "just to keep an eye on things." But by that time, she had been a thorn in the side of the landfill developers since the late 1990s.

In those days, Canadian Waste Services owned the landfill and they had singled out for increased attention residents living within one kilometre of the site—about forty people from twenty-five households—and invited them to the so-called kitchen table meetings. IER Planning, Research and Management Services, a consulting firm based in Concord, Ontario, was retained by the waste company to facilitate the consultation program. Perhaps IER believed that small-group discussions in a home setting would result in more personal interactions, and thus elicit the co-operation of the residents most affected by the landfill expansion. Thirteen or so meetings were organized by IER, with company staff or their consultants providing information and inviting comments and questions.

Margaret, remember, went to only one such meeting. She saw them as a sham. Alarm bells were already ringing in her head. Margaret was afraid of leachate from a bigger dump migrating through fissures in the rock and contaminating area wells, including perhaps her own. At the time, there was already a Public Liaison Committee consisting of landfill officials, municipal representatives, and community members. With the expansion project, an Environmental Advisory Committee was formed so that community members and officials from the municipalities of Greater Napanee and Tyendinaga Township and the Mohawks of the Bay of Quinte could sit down with the company and its consultants to discuss the terms of reference—a legal formality required by the provincial government before any dump expansion could be entertained. Initially held separately, the meetings of the two committees were later held jointly and made open to the public. The deputy reeve for Tyendinaga Township was supposed to attend these meetings but did not, so Margaret began going in his place.

One day, company officials phoned to say they wanted to meet with her alone. Three men came around to visit Margaret in her township office. The first thing she did was to insist that the township clerk be there to witness any such conversation. The second was to decline company carrots. "I said no," she told me, "to their offer to fix township roads, and I said no to their offer of personal favours." The visitors left angry, Margaret recalls, muttering among themselves. They said that other communities did accept such offers. Napanee, Margaret told me that day, received funds for the hospital and for a new sports centre, while Deseronto had its hockey team looked after.

Margaret emphasizes that the alliances formed in the early days of the landfill fight were critical to any success in combatting this unwanted development. By 2005, the CCCTE had formed and some major players on the *no* side had emerged—Steve Geneja and Allan Gardiner, for example. Steve Geneja, the former deputy land registrar for nearby Hastings County, would become an active member of the citizens' group opposing the landfill expansion. Allan Gardiner, who lived on a farm near the dump, would over the course of many years chair several environmental and community organizations opposed to the landfill expansion.

One measure of the passage of time in this protracted battle is that Margaret's good friend Steve Geneja, a frail and elderly man in a nursing home, died in January 2016. Pilot Howard O'Connor, a passionate dump opponent, died in 2013. Allan Gardiner is also gone; he died in 2013 after devoting a big chunk of his life to this issue. Allan had been there from the beginning in 1988 when the first expansion of the old Sutcliffe dumpsite was approved. He was an extraordinary resource. Allan was the memory bank in which the history of the dump fight had been deposited, and over the years of gathering material for this work, I would call on him again and again.

***

The Mohawks of the Bay of Quinte remain attentive to the landfill issue. "That a friendship and alliance formed with the Mohawks over this issue was huge," Margaret Walsh says. It struck me what a progressive person she is. In the old days, she told me, people looked down on the Indians and hired them to do dirty work such as digging ditches. "I looked up to the Mohawks—they have been here a long time, long before we were here," she said. "I am grateful to them."

Her quiet manner belied her effectiveness in a leadership role but, as it turned out, she was the one who started the ball rolling for the dump opposition movement. For more than a year, Margaret had regularly attended the evening meetings on the landfill expansion organized by Canadian Waste Services. She became increasingly sceptical and concerned about the information dispensed by the company and its consultants. She suspected that the proponent was not giving the nearby communities the true facts about the expansion and its impacts, but was instead giving them a version designed to win community support and co-operation. If the potential effects could be mitigated and the company had the expertise to implement the program, as residents had been assured, why wouldn't they want a landfill? Especially if, according to company spokesperson Kevin Bechard, it came with "about twenty-one hundred direct jobs and thousands of related service providers"?[4]

Margaret Walsh never believed those numbers, nor did anyone on the *no* side. When she arranged a gathering of local residents for February 8, 1999, Margaret believed it was important to invite the Mohawks of nearby Tyendinaga Mohawk Territory. At that time, there was little contact between the local white population and the Mohawk community. Margaret did not even know whom to contact, but she did pass the word around, encouraging everyone to get the message to the Mohawks.

On a cold Monday night, more than a hundred residents turned up at Melrose Hall in Tyendinaga Township. They included Andrew Maracle, a Mohawk Elder known as the storyteller. He was also an ordained Christian minister and a tireless advocate for Indigenous rights. Invited to speak to the group, he stood up and talked about the obligation of every Mohawk to preserve Mother Earth. He emphasized everyone's obligation to leave as few footprints as possible on the land, and he described a Mohawk family going out for a walk on a snowy day. The father walked in front, and the mother came behind him and placed her feet in his footsteps in the snow. The children followed, planting their feet in the imprints left by the father and mother. Maracle ended by saying that he himself would soon be walking with the greatest man who ever walked the earth.

He finished to loud applause. Maracle had barely taken his seat again when he suddenly collapsed. Someone nearby caught him before he fell.

Margaret, who had been reeve all of two weeks, was at a loss to know what to do. Firefighters from the firehall across the street as well as nurses at the meeting attempted to revive him and an ambulance was called, but Maracle was pronounced dead shortly after arrival at Belleville General Hospital. He was eighty-five.

Maracle's collapse had a profound effect. The meeting soon adjourned. Everyone went home, some thinking that the incident was a bad omen. But Mike Bossio, a Tyendinaga Township councillor, said he felt the meeting was a positive one. The gathering appeared to solidify opposition to the landfill, and attendees had formed a new group, the Stop the Richmond Dump Expansion Citizens' Committee. Moreover, members of the Mohawk community had come to the meeting and would soon become actively involved. This meeting marked the beginning of an opposition movement. Actually, recalled Margaret, there had been another one over ten years earlier that was spearheaded by Allan Gardiner. That was a confrontation between residents and Tricil, the Sutcliffe family, and the Ministry of the Environment. At that time, an uneasy peace had been forged between the residents and the company, which Allan attributed to a considerate and competent landfill manager.

As I listened to Margaret recounting all this, I wondered whether her involvement in the dump issue ever hurt her at the polls. She had stood with placard-carrying protesters on the streets of Napanee, and several times—on her own dime, she hastens to add—went with delegations to Queen's Park to press their case against the landfill expansion. Such militancy is uncommon in Loyalist Napanee and environs. "I never lost votes because of my involvement in the dump issue," Margaret assured me. "I probably gained a few."

She did, however, lose sleep on occasion. At one point, around 2005, during a county meeting Margaret made comments about the dump issue while a reporter from the *Belleville Intelligencer* was in attendance. She made the point that Waste Management was perhaps not the ideal company for the job. Those comments were then used by another newspaper, the *Tweed News*, in a revised piece. A few days later a fax arrived at the Tyendinaga Township office: Margaret Walsh was being threatened by Waste Management.

"I thought they would sue me or the township, for I was reeve at the time," Margaret recalled, "and I was petrified. I could not sleep some nights, fearing they would ruin me—but I was also concerned for the next generation. For two weeks I was helpless. I was so upset. I was going crazy." As advised by township officials, Margaret sent Waste Management's threatening letter to the township lawyer, but she heard nothing back for two weeks. Beset with worry, she contemplated retiring from her position as reeve. Finally, she met with her own lawyer, who examined the articles in the two newspapers.

"Waste Management has no case," the lawyer assured Margaret. "I'll just fax them and tell them that any further correspondence should come to me." No further correspondence came. And that was the end of that. But the incident made a lasting impression.

Margaret retired as reeve in 2010, but she continued to be a part of any citizen activity connected with the dump. When the province's Environmental Review Tribunal held sessions in Belleville and Tyendinaga Township during the spring of 2015, she attended many of them, often in the company of Chief Don Maracle. They had a history. When the chief ran for re-election in December 2013, she had waited with him into the small hours of the night to watch the tabulations come in. A political alliance had morphed into a close, personal relationship—something that happened to many of those engaged in this fight.

Reeve Margaret Walsh (Tyendinaga Township) and Mohawk Chief Don Maracle urging Greater Napanee town council to support opposition to dump expansion (October 24, 2000). Photo courtesy of the *Napanee Beaver*.

Margaret's abiding concern through all these years was the children of the community, including her own three grandchildren. Contaminated air and water from an ever-expanding dumpsite, Margaret worried, imperilled those youngsters and the next generation of children.

"No one knows what health effects that could have in the future on these people, especially the children," Margaret told a packed meeting of Napanee Town Council in 2008 when the landfill expansion was once more on the agenda. Her own township of Tyendinaga, along with nearby Hastings County and the city of Belleville, were shipping their garbage to Laflèche Environmental, a landfill site near Cornwall in eastern Ontario that was a geologically safe and viable alternative. Margaret had taken regional officials to the site, which was set on nine metres of red clay. Here was an ideal site for a landfill. The Richmond Landfill, on the other hand, was set on fractured limestone, a geological phrase that every citizen opposed to expanding Fred Sutcliffe's old dump came to know well.

For Waste Management, the old dump—"half a mile from the 401," as Margaret put it—was too tempting to pass up. It was easily accessible from Toronto, Belleville, Prince Edward County, Kingston, and other municipalities in between. And money could be made from picking up and storing garbage. One of the last questions I put to Margaret before leaving with an armful of banana muffins was about Fred Sutcliffe. I had talked to another key player in the dump battle, Mary Lynne Sammon, just before she died early in 2015. Though Mary Lynne very much opposed dump expansion, she expressed some sympathy for Fred Sutcliffe. She thought he was doing what he thought best for his family. Did Margaret, I asked, likewise feel for Sutcliffe?

"No," replied Margaret with some emotion. "He got rich selling the land to the company."

Then I asked Margaret, based on her experience, to offer her best advice to a community facing a threat such as a dump expansion. The burden of her counsel was, get help and organize. "Get good engineers," she said. "Build a committee. Ian Munro, for example, is an engineer. Steve Medd is a geologist. We had several learned men and women working for us, and that made a difference. Get some experts on your side."

Passing through a sunroom to exit the Walsh farmhouse, I noticed that Margaret's walls were full of photographs of family, including a great many of her three children and three grandchildren. This, I thought, is how Margaret had retained her resolve through all those years of fighting company people and their hollow reassurances.

CHAPTER 5

GOODBYE LOCAL GARBAGEMAN, HELLO MEGA-DUMP

"Nothing will change except the colour of the vehicles."
—George Reddom, Tricil spokesperson, upon buying
Sutcliffe's dumpsite, 1988

In September 1985, approximately thirty-one years after he started collecting garbage, Fred Sutcliffe submitted an application to the provincial Ministry of the Environment to expand his dumpsite northwest of Napanee. This is when the trouble started.

The community had heard rumours that Sutcliffe was applying to increase the area and capacity of his dumpsite. Some neighbours were perplexed because they knew that such a large expansion required substantial funding and that Sutcliffe did not have that kind of money. Soon enough, they found out more from Sutcliffe himself. People noticed the familiar figure—tall, thin, and bald—going around knocking on doors. He informed his neighbours that he had applied for approval to expand his dumpsite—but only for the small area and dumping space (130 metres) he had lost when the Ontario Hydro corridor went through his property and towers were erected.

Neighbours, trusting what he told them, were not concerned. In hindsight, they should have been greatly concerned; Sutcliffe's version of the facts was a gross misrepresentation. He also did not disclose one crucial point: he was in the process of negotiating the sale of Sutcliffe Sanitation Services to a major waste management company. When the truth was revealed about a year later, Sutcliffe's neighbours voiced outrage.

Much had changed since Fred Sutcliffe began collecting garbage in Richmond Township in 1954. When provincial licensing became mandatory in 1971, he applied for and received a Provincial Certificate of Approval for a waste disposal site of 3.6 hectares (9.0 acres) at an annual rate of 15,000 tonnes. By the 1980s, expansion of a waste disposal facility in Ontario required government approval, and in September 1985, Sutcliffe applied for an expansion. His application was referred to the Environmental Assessment Board—an independent, quasi-judicial body—for a public hearing.

The board had held a preliminary meeting in December 1985 to discuss issues relating to the Sutcliffe application. Citizens in the townships of Richmond and Tyendinaga and the Mohawks of the Bay of Quinte were generally not aware of any posted notices, and neither did they receive any by mail. Since they had no knowledge of this meeting, none attended.

The following month, early in January 1986, the public hearing to consider the Sutcliffe application was scheduled. Sutcliffe was seeking to expand his dumpsite from 3.6 hectares (9 acres) to 16.2 hectares (40 acres) and an annual rate increase from 15,000 tonnes to 125,000 tonnes for a period of nineteen to twenty-four years. The central issue before the board, and likely the principal reason the Sutcliffe application was referred to a public hearing, was the hydrogeological suitability of the site. Would the proposed expansion impact the environment, especially surface water and groundwater?

Engineering consultants Brian Beatty and Franklin Ford represented Sutcliffe Sanitation at the hearing. Barry Burns, Cyril Holland, and John Bishop represented the Ministry of the Environment.

Beatty estimated that about 1 per cent of the leachate generated from the landfill area would enter the bedrock, and that its vertical penetration to the groundwater would be insignificant. On the other hand, he expected that leachate production from a new expanded landfill site would be twice what it was at the existing dumpsite.

Beatty indicated there was a leachate plume—that is, leachate that has migrated into groundwater—extending about 140 to 150 metres north of the landfill area at a depth of about seven metres. He estimated that the leachate was moving at a rate of ten metres per year, and he expected that it would expand to the north and west. Eventually it could reach the cattail marsh at the point where Marysville Creek crosses the western boundary of the Sutcliffe property. He expected that the groundwater flow from the upper reaches of the watershed would dilute the leachate plume before it reached the marsh, so that contaminants would reach near background levels.

Beatty had not taken samples of the leachate and did not know its actual strength, but he believed it was weak. He expected the leachate to be almost at levels found in the surrounding environment as it travelled further from its source. In his view, the impact of the leachate on the water quality of Marysville Creek was insignificant.

In the final analysis, Beatty concluded, the patterns and conditions of groundwater flow at the site rendered it suitable for waste disposal. He believed that the design and operation of the site would ensure that leachate production was minimized to rates that could be assimilated on-site with no threat to neighbouring water supplies. He proposed a monitoring program to ensure that water resources would be protected.

Cyril Holland, the ministry's surface water evaluator, disagreed with Beatty's conclusions concerning the rate of groundwater flow. He thought the plume might be moving at a rate three to four times faster than that estimated by Beatty. He was also concerned about the lack of data regarding the contaminant strengths of the pure, undiluted leachate. He stressed that it was important to know the leachate strength in order to be sure that the dilution Beatty had proposed would occur in the bedrock.

Holland identified two discharge zones in the area where groundwater emerges to the surface—one in the cattail marsh on the Sutcliffe property and another in the area west of County Road 10. These two zones could experience some impacts from groundwater contamination, he said, as they received contributions from groundwater.

Holland agreed with Beatty's contention that the site had natural attenuation for diminishing or eliminating leachate components and that it was therefore suitable for landfilling. However, he predicted that while the leachate contaminants travelling to Marysville Creek might presently be at acceptable levels, those levels were likely to become unacceptable with the proposed landfill expansion.

Barry Burns, the ministry's surface water engineer, agreed that although there had been only a minor impact on the quality of water in Marysville Creek to date, there was a definite possibility of greater impacts in the future. He cautioned that careful monitoring of the creek was essential to ensure that contaminant levels did not exceed the ministry's standards at any point in the stream, not just within the boundaries of the Sutcliffe property.

Monitoring of surface waters should be ongoing, he stated. Beatty, in contrast, had proposed monthly monitoring for a two-year period and then only when impacts were identified. Burns recommended that background levels for water quality be established by monitoring wells at some distance from the landfill.

Despite the concerns raised by Holland and Burns, the board concluded that the hydrogeology of the site was suitable for waste disposal and recommended approval for the expansion.

***

Although notice of the January 1986 "public" hearing appeared in the local newspaper, the *Napanee Beaver*, no one in the community had paid much heed to it. This was in part because Fred Sutcliffe had already conveyed to them in person what they thought was the essential information about his planned expansion. It was also in part because Sutcliffe was well liked and generally regarded as a good garbageman and a good neighbour. No one saw any reason to question the information he had passed on to them in his visits. Mostly busy farmers, they had little interest in what they thought would be technical discussions of expansion plans. As a result, even though some people knew about the hearing, not a single member of the community showed up to comment on Sutcliffe's application.

Not knowing that Sutcliffe's application had requested an *eightfold* increase in disposal capacity, most people in the community thought that the situation would remain much as it had been before. However, events took an unexpected turn at the hearing. This would have devastating effects on the community.

Fred Sutcliffe had submitted an application for approval of a service area made up of selected municipalities in four counties—Lennox and Addington, Hastings, Prince Edward, and Frontenac—within a radius of fifty kilometres of the site. But at some point during the proceedings, and with the concurrence of the Ministry of the Environment, Sutcliffe amended the application to increase the service area to include "all municipalities in the Province of Ontario."[5] Not one resident was there to protest this change, but soon after debate swirled in the community. Was the enormous increase in the service area a permissible or even an ethical amendment on the part of the board? People in the area were not aware that they could have appealed the board's decision merely on that basis. Moreover, the appeal had to be submitted within twenty-eight days of the board's release of its decision, but Sutcliffe's neighbours knew none of this either. They simply felt betrayed and angry. If indeed there was fairness, some said, the board would have adjourned the hearing, advised them of the amendment, and resumed at a later date. Were there no objections, the amendment could have been allowed to stand. Otherwise, they believed, it should have been disallowed.

Following the hearing, there was intense speculation as to who was behind the amendment and why board and ministry officials had supported the applicant. Residents did not believe that it was Sutcliffe's idea to expand the service area to include all Ontario municipalities; had this been the case, that request would have been part of his initial application. The prevailing hypothesis was that Sutcliffe was prompted to make the amendment by Tricil, the major Sarnia-based waste management company that was then negotiating with the Sutcliffe family to purchase the dumpsite and operation.

Only in hindsight did neighbours begin to imagine how the pieces of the puzzle might have fitted together. Tricil would finance the proposed dump expansion while providing funds for Sutcliffe to hire the engineering consultants required to support the plan. The company would also guide Sutcliffe through the application process and the hearing process—if and when the application was referred to a public hearing.

They speculated that Tricil was not interested in operating a local municipal dumpsite, and the sale of the Sutcliffe operation was therefore contingent on approval of the dump expansion. If the expansion had not received approval at the hearing, Tricil would likely have cut its losses and walked away from the sale, leaving Sutcliffe to continue collecting garbage for his neighbours. Although no one had any evidence or proof that money had actually changed hands, this version of events circulated within the small rural community. Eventually, the story died down as other subjects, now more interesting, came to the fore.

While some board members expressed reservations about waste coming in from all municipalities across Ontario and registered concern about potential groundwater contamination, the board had nonetheless recommended approval of the proposed expansion. A Provisional Certificate of Approval for a Waste Disposal Site was issued to Sutcliffe Sanitation Services Ltd. in August 1987.

On December 30 of that year, the Sutcliffe family completed the sale of their farm and waste operation to Tricil. Soon after, the company called an information meeting to announce that it would be managing Sutcliffe's dumpsite, now known as the Richmond Landfill. Referring to conditions of sale between the two parties, Tricil spokesperson George Reddom said, "We can't disclose financial information because we are a private company, not on the stock exchange. There's a fair amount of work required to bring the Deseronto landfill site at Deseronto Road and Highway 401 up to provincial Ministry of Environment standards." He assured the company's future clients that "Napanee's waste disposal and pick-up services will not be altered under the management of Tricil Ltd. Nothing will change except the colour of the vehicles."[6]

After the sale, Fred and Mary Sutcliffe relocated to Tyendinaga Township, where they owned a house and kept a herd of cattle. The couple lived quietly at this farm and did not associate with neighbours. Fred would die in 1999 and Mary in 2006, at the ages of eighty-four and eighty-nine, respectively.

***

Many of those who had grown up in the area believed that allowing the dump to expand was a grave error. They were soon proven right. Marysville Creek had been a place where children went to play. The water was clear and it was an excellent place to find fish and frogs, or just to splash in the water. The cattail marsh adjacent to County Road 10 (also known as Deseronto Road; locals call it Boundary Road, as it formed the western boundary of Richmond Township) was another place parents took their children to—especially on hot summer days. The cool water was fed by underground springs. At the corner where Boundary Road intersects with Selby Road was a swamp where full-grown hard maple trees grew in the water. A tributary of Marysville Creek drains this swamp. The brilliant fall colours of the swamp maples reminded residents that another season was passing and winter would soon come.

Dead swamp maples on east side of Deseronto Road (County Road 10).
Photo courtesy of Lutz Forkert.

Within a few years of the dump expansion, Marysville Creek became a dead stream, and the fish, frogs, and other aquatic life disappeared. Rick Shelley, who grew up in the area and now farms nearby, sadly recalled to me, "I would go down to Marysville Creek to catch minnows. There were so many I could scoop them up with my hands. Now, there's not a single one. I was going to show my grandchildren what I used to do at the creek when I was a boy. Not a chance. It's all gone now."

The water in the creek turned murky and became choked with weeds. The cattail marsh died, and the cattails, too, were replaced with weeds.

Most devastating to the residents was that the hard maples in the swamp also died, first on the east side of the road, the same side as the landfill, and then on the west side. All that remained were stumps; the seasonal changes of colours were a thing of the past.

During the board hearing, Holland and Burns from the ministry had predicted impacts of the proposed expansion on Marysville Creek, the cat-tail marsh, and the groundwater discharge area west of County Road 10. Despite this, they concluded that the site was suitable for waste disposal and recommended approval of the expansion. A critical topic that did not receive sufficient attention at the board hearing was the fractured lime-stone underlying the proposed site, and the impossibility of tracking leach-ate that may be percolating underground and into the groundwater. Due to potential leachate impacts on groundwater, fractured limestone is possibly one of the most hazardous geological conditions for storing garbage; this topic would be a matter of considerable debate in days and years to come.

Area residents believe that approval of the expansion should never have been allowed. They strongly believe that the Ministry of the Environment, mandated to protect the environment in Ontario, failed them in every way. The expanded landfill has polluted their land, their water, and their air.

CHAPTER 6

FIRST STIRRINGS OF ANGER

"We welcomed you, and you sat at our dinner table.
Look at what you have done to us."
—Winnifred Jackson addressing Fred Sutcliffe, 1988

On January 2, 1988, Tricil Ltd. took over Sutcliffe Sanitation Services and renamed it the Richmond Landfill. The company's promise that nothing would change but the colour of the trucks rapidly proved hollow.

Almost immediately, there was an exponential increase in the amounts of residential and commercial garbage being trucked into the site. Loads were now coming from all over Ontario—from Trenton, Belleville, Deseronto, Picton, and other communities. There were more and bigger trucks, more traffic noise, more dust, fumes, and pollution. Township roads soon showed signs of deterioration, with garbage flying off the trucks and strewn along the roadsides.

Allan Gardiner, who lived and farmed on three hundred acres three kilometres from the landfill, was disturbed by the changes. He had been suspicious of the events that had taken place at the Environmental Assessment Board hearing in 1986, and, like his neighbours, very much regretted not having attended. He wondered whether what had transpired at the meeting had brought the disruptions to his community.

In January 1988, Allan drove to the Kingston offices of the Ministry of the Environment, where he persuaded a reluctant official to give him a copy of both the board report and the Provisional Certificate of Approval.[7] As he read the two documents, he was horrified to learn that Sutcliffe Sanitation Services had gotten approval to receive 125,000 tonnes of waste from all municipalities in Ontario. His idyllic life in the country, and that of the community, was in the process of changing drastically. He promptly informed his neighbours of the mountain of garbage that was forming.

Allan circulated copies of the two documents. Neighbours erupted in anger and started talking to one another. Rick Shelley recalled that some of his neighbours gathered for a fish fry at the home of Gary Tucker, who owned eighty acres not far from the landfill site. Rick remembered some of the people who were there: Allan and Iris Gardiner, Don and Christine

Shelley, Jack Stewart, Don Stafford, Tim Shelley, and Helen and Grant Kimmerly. After much discussion, they agreed it was time to formalize the opposition by creating a committee. They knew that, if they were to have an effective voice, they needed to galvanize the whole community.

About thirty-five people living near the landfill site met during the first week of February 1988. "Our main concern was with the increased volume of garbage, especially from outside our general area, coming to the site," said Allan. "We were worried about a decrease in land values in the area, the pollution of private wells, increased traffic, and damage to local roads. One resident at the meeting said he had seen someone attempting to dump a half-ton of waste on private property because the driver claimed he couldn't afford Tricil's increased prices."[8] They formed an ad hoc committee that consisted of three people from each township: Allan Gardiner, Peter Johnson, and Bert Winter from Richmond Township, and Jack Stewart, Don Stafford, and Gary Tucker from Tyendinaga Township. The committee was called Richmond/Tyendinaga Environmental Association, and Allan Gardiner was elected chair. A week later, this small group of residents organized a dump meeting that was attended by many in their community.

Nearby residents were not the only ones upset with Tricil. After assurances that the company would not alter waste disposal and pickup services, people assumed that prices would also remain unchanged. They recalled that the company's spokesperson had said "only the colour of the vehicles" would change. But now Tricil quoted the local Canadian Tire store a 200 per cent price increase to pick up the contents of its forty-cubic-yard waste disposal bin each week.[9] Fred Sutcliffe had been charging $75 for that pickup; the new price was $225. The store manager and others like him at first refused to sign the new contracts. But eventually they relented; they had no choice.

Residents in the vicinity scraped together enough money to hire a lawyer, Robert Scott from Belleville, in an attempt to get the ministry's approval of the dump expansion overturned. A date was set for a meeting to discuss the new development, and notice was sent around the community—including to the Mohawks of the Bay of Quinte in the nearby reserve, downstream of the landfill. Although the farmers had not associated much with the Mohawk community, the organizers believed it was necessary to get as many people out as possible.

On February 16, 1988, area residents met in the basement of Empey Hill United Church, the church adjacent to the dumpsite.[10] Present were their lawyer, Robert Scott; the former owner of the dumpsite, Fred Sutcliffe, and his son Fred Sutcliffe Jr.; and Sylvio Richard, regional manager of Tricil.

Brian Beatty, the engineering consultant who had represented Sutcliffe Sanitation Services at the board hearing, was there now as a consultant for Tricil. John Bishop, the environment ministry's area manager in eastern Ontario, had represented the ministry at the board hearing; he was also there. The church hall was filled to capacity, with more than two hundred people in attendance, some of them forced to stand outside.

The meeting was highly emotional. An elderly community member, Winnifred Jackson, addressed Fred Sutcliffe Sr.: "You came to this country as an immigrant. We welcomed you, and you sat at our dinner table. Look at what you have done to us." Sylvio Richard of Tricil assured her that she didn't have anything to worry about. But people there were both worried and extremely angry with the Sutcliffe family, with Tricil, and with the ministry. Some recalled that for many years, Sutcliffe Sanitation had collected garbage from Richmond Township and the Town of Napanee without any complaints. In fact, the Sutcliffes were regarded as good neighbours who were rendering a much-needed service. But that had all changed.

People were concerned about their environment and their health. Don Stafford, a member of the newly formed environmental association, pointed out that testing for water quality was incomplete and did not meet the criteria set out in the province's Provisional Certificate of Approval granted to Sutcliffe Sanitation. For example, testing of private wells in the area showed levels of phenols—toxic compounds found naturally but also manufactured for production of plastics and other applications—higher than the maximum allowable levels. Stafford was concerned, as his own well was only about thirty metres from Marysville Creek, whose headwaters originated at the landfill.

John Bishop admitted that phenol was known to be present in the area at levels higher than normal, and that this was a problem. Admitting there was a need to carry out further tests, he emphasized that the ministry had a program in place for the testing. Brian Beatty noted that phenols occurred naturally at the site, and that every well drilled in the area of the dump contained phenol. Allan Gardiner questioned the wisdom of expanding the dumpsite at the present location when phenol levels were already high in the area.

Beatty responded that he had never seen an impact that he was concerned about: Tricil had numerous monitoring wells on the site to track the movement of leachate. He said that if there were a serious impact, a detailed contingency plan would be deployed. This would involve the construction of a pipe to collect the leachate and pump it into storage ponds or lagoons. The leachate would then be used to irrigate the landfill—that is, it would be sprayed onto the waste mound.

This was possibly the worst solution for dealing with leachate, and it would come back to bite. Recirculation of leachate is a strategy used to save on costs that would otherwise be incurred for treating the leachate before disposal or for disposal at a local sewage treatment plant. This method of dealing with leachate concentrates the leachate and its constituents. Should it migrate off-site, the impacts are likely to be more serious, as contaminants are present at greater concentrations. This would be borne out later, when leachate from the landfill was indeed identified off-site.

Beatty pointed out that Tricil was required to sample and test surface water twice a year, but he said he would recommend to the company that sampling be carried out more frequently, especially during spring runoff.

Residents were rightly concerned about contamination of their drinking water with phenol—my own research had revealed that it is classified as a substance with potential toxic effects.[11] Phenol is an irritant, and studies have shown increased incidence of diarrhea, mouth sores, and irritation of the mouth in individuals exposed to drinking water containing phenol.[12] Long-term exposure to phenol can cause liver damage and heart disease. Residents thought that Beatty or Bishop should, at least, have offered to test for phenols in their well water to determine if the chemical was indeed present, even if it was at levels they should not be concerned about.

Some residents noted that the garbage was not covered by six inches (fifteen centimetres) of soil at the end of the day as required. The Tricil spokesperson responded that he was aware of only one occasion when the garbage was left uncovered due to equipment failure. However, some at the meeting were adamant that there were more occasions and that they had photographs to confirm it.

Residents were most angry about an infestation of rats in the area. Mary Blair, who lived directly north of the dump on Selby Road, said she had never encountered rats previously, but now they were destroying parts of her house. "My son is afraid to go downstairs at night. You can hear them moving the food around in the kitchen cupboards." Another neighbour, Ethel McKnight, said she had spent $70 in 1987 and $77 in just the first six weeks of 1988 on rat poison to control the vermin invading her home. Sylvio Richard replied that he was not aware of the problem, but Tricil would be willing to make arrangements to send pest control people around the neighbourhood to attend to it.[13]

People were upset with Tricil and the Sutcliffes, but they were especially furious with the Ministry of the Environment. They believed that it was the responsibility of the regulator not only to license but also to adequately monitor the operation of the landfill. They expected the ministry to ensure that the landfill owner complied with the conditions imposed by the Provisional Certificate of Approval.

"You can hear them moving the food around in the kitchen cupboards."
Mary Blair complains about rats invading her home at dump
protest meeting at Empey Hill church (February 16, 1988).
Photo courtesy of the Community Archives of Belleville and Hastings
County (Intelligencer Fonds).

An issue that raised considerable ire was the hearings of the Environmental Assessment Board on the landfill expansion. The preliminary hearing had been held in December 1985 and the public hearing in January 1986. Chief Earl Hill of the Tyendinaga Mohawk Territory, who came to the meeting with a few residents of the reserve, asked, "Why weren't we consulted?" He wanted an answer. "We are downstream [of Marysville Creek] and we want to make damn sure our well water is okay." The chief had received no notification of the hearings.

The ministry spokesperson replied that notice of the public hearings had been placed in the local newspaper, the *Napanee Beaver*. It was pointed out that not everyone received or read the local newspaper; this was particularly the case in the Mohawk community. Bishop maintained that the "notice was legitimate in law." He emphasized that no one came to the meeting to oppose the expansion. Allan Gardiner explained that the complacency of the residents at the time of the hearings was due, in part, to the cordial relationship between neighbours and the Sutcliffe family.

They were regarded as good neighbours, and there was no reason to believe that things would be any different in the future. "It's the way country people think," Allan said. "Our elected representatives should have protected us, if not legally, then morally."

Robert Scott, the solicitor for the Richmond/Tyendinaga Environmental Association, asked Bishop if the ministry would reopen the hearings. Bishop replied, "Based on my understanding of the law—no." Scott then requested that Tricil officials join the citizens in requesting the ministry to reopen the hearings. Tricil declined. Bishop suggested instead that a Public Liaison Committee be constituted, chaired by someone from the association, with representatives from the ministry and Tricil.

Scott countered, "The citizens do not want a dump at all." He then challenged Bishop, "The working face has not been covered, and criteria have not been met. Do something. Lay charges."

After the meeting, Bishop voiced his disappointment at the lack of interest in a liaison committee. But residents were too frustrated and angry with municipal officials, Tricil officials, and ministry representatives to have anything to do with them. They were also angry that Richmond Township's council had let them down so badly. Questioned by a reporter about the council's role in supporting the landfill expansion, Reeve Gary Hartin's answer was, "We sent our planner and our clerk to the hearings. I spent some time there myself. Our feeling at the time was that we needed to secure a dumpsite for the future of Napanee and Richmond and some of our neighbours." He was not supportive of a move to reopen the hearings. "We have to live with it, keep the association active and pressure the government to legislate alternatives to landfill such as recycling." But when Hartin retired after twelve years on council, he said, "If I had to say I made two mistakes on council, one of them would be giving [Fred] Sutcliffe the license to take garbage from all of Ontario..."[14]

People left the meeting feeling more worried than before. They now realized that they could not depend on their government to protect them. Had they been naive to think otherwise?

"Those were early days," Allan Gardiner told me, "and we had no idea then how much worse it could get." He recalled the early events of the dump fight for me when I came on the scene. "That would come ten years later when another company—Canadian Waste Services—became the owner of the Richmond Landfill. We could not possibly have imagined the ensuing nightmare or that the dump issue would consume our lives for such a long time—decades, it turned out."

***

One day while we were waiting for the minister's decision on the landfill expansion, Allan Gardiner drove me around to show me various features of the area, including the groundwater recharge and discharge areas. We stopped at the cemetery where Fred Sutcliffe Sr. was buried. Standing by the gravestone, Allan said, "There lies the man who started it all." He paused for a moment before adding, "How different my life would have been had he not come here and had the dump not been here."

Allan was, however, resigned. "I did what I had to do," he said. I asked what he would have done had the dump expansion not come to this area. He said that he would have led a quiet life with his family and grandchildren and tended to his cows and hens—he had some rare breeds, and the eggs he brought me had the creamiest yolks I ever tasted. He would also have liked to have had time to do more writing—Alan liked to read and write, but the dump had scuttled that one. It was during our forays into the countryside that I saw a gentle side to the big man that was well camouflaged by an explosive temper—a loud voice, arm-waving, and bulging eyes. Only those who had been involved in the dump fight from its early days would realize how much this man had sacrificed.

CHAPTER 7

AN UNWAVERING ACTIVIST

*"Children living near the dump were throwing up while waiting for the school bus.
As a mother of twelve, it really bothered me."*
—CCCTE member Mary Lynne Sammon, January 2015

To be successful, every activist organization needs a secretary cum researcher cum historian to take notes at meetings and generate the minutes while providing context and background, someone dogged and meticulous and fuelled by outrage. Someone to sort the paper trail, because it's certain that a big company's first strategy is to bombard outraged citizens with reports, studies, documents, and assurances from paid experts that all will be well. For the citizens who opposed the transformation of the Richmond Landfill into a mega-dump, Mary Lynne Sammon was that person for almost two decades.

I say *was* because, sadly, Mary Lynne died in January 2015—just days after I went to see her at Lennox and Addington County General Hospital in Napanee. She was in the palliative care unit, dressed in a blue hospital gown and sitting up in bed. The strawberry blond hair, glasses, and striking grey eyes were all familiar, but the muted tone and faint smile were not. I had spent countless hours with Mary Lynne in the Napanee Land Registry office and at the Lennox and Addington Museum and Archives as we tracked severances and land transfers and Waste Management's land acquisitions over the years. I knew her to be a tireless and ebullient woman with an easy laugh. The woman who faced me from that hospital bed was more sombre. Mary Lynne was still sharp, still able to call up moments from her dump fight, but now she had a much bigger contest on her hands.

Mary Lynne had been diagnosed with lung cancer late in 2014 and told she had about two to three months to live. What a shock it was to her and her family, and to all of us in her corner. She had gone in to see her doctor about a persistent cough and, after some tests, was given the devastating news. "It's not over till it's over," she told me on the phone, "and I'm going to try my darndest to make sure it's not going to be over that soon."

"I'm still optimistic," Mary Lynne said that day in hospital. But she said it with little conviction. We both knew that she was in the palliative care unit, but she acted as though that was not the case; maybe that was the best way to deal with the situation. Or perhaps she was generously sparing me from having to confront the obvious—that she was dying. I knew she wanted to be at home, but that was not feasible, as her family could not manage to care for her. But she was comfortable. "If you have to be in a hospital," she said, "this is where you should come. The nursing care is superb and the food is good."

That day she did not look unwell, but she had lost a lot of weight and there were times when she would drift off, go somewhere private in her thoughts. I would respect those silences and give her a moment to collect herself, and then return to the subject at hand.

Very much like Margaret Walsh, another grandmother and fellow activist, Mary Lynne was moved to join the dump expansion fight because of the threat that a mega-dump posed to the local environment and thus to local children. When she observed children covering their noses as they stood outside, or heard about children throwing up while waiting for the school bus, she was furious. Mary Lynne worried for those children. "I probably lost sleep over that issue," she told me. "Air quality: that is the one thing that most incensed me."

Mary Lynne loved her children and they clearly loved her. That day in the hospital she told me how overwhelmed she was by their generosity.

"It's been amazing," Mary Lynne remarked. "The kids came home at Christmas. They cleaned up the house and bought me all new furniture, instead of all the stuff I had accumulated over the years." It was one of the first things she talked about. They had come home from all over—Kansas, Nova Scotia, British Columbia, and London, England—to say a final good-bye to their mother.

That's what struck me most about Mary Lynne. Her gratitude for kindness shown, her upbeat nature. She talked, for example, about the master ceramicist Harlan House, who lives in the village of Lonsdale, on the banks of the Salmon River—a waterway residents worried would be imperilled by leachate from the dump. House is a much decorated and much admired artist whose work is featured in museums and art galleries all over the world. Mary Lynne was taken aback that someone of his stature would donate his artwork—four ceramic pieces and a water colour painting, altogether a value of eleven thousand dollars—that were a key component in the fundraising efforts of anti-dump activists. Those pieces of art were the focus of a raffle ticket campaign that raised almost thirty thousand dollars. Many, including Mary Lynne, made a huge effort to sell as many raffle tickets as possible. If the general wisdom was that getting experts on your side was key to victory, here was its corollary: getting a prominent artist on your side isn't a bad idea either.

"It's amazing how generous people are," said Mary Lynne as she remembered that moment. "We raised so much money—and a lot of it was donations."

Unlike most big city hospitals, the recently renovated county hospital in Napanee offers some beds—including the palliative care beds—on the ground floor. This means that the ample floor-to-ceiling windows in Mary Lynne's room afforded views of nearby grass and trees. That greenery, she said, was important to her.

Mary Lynne was enthusiastic about offering stories and advice to community groups facing their own unwanted development, and passed on to me much information and many stories, as well as the history of the prolonged war. I am grateful for that and will miss her, for she was a friend and an important lifeline to the community. Although I spent a lot of time with Mary Lynne, we had mostly been preoccupied with dump matters and had not talked much about her personal life. She did, however, tell me that she had twelve children. In response to my incredulous expression, she simply said, "I love children." But now it was time for us to talk about those details. I started by asking about her background.

"I taught school for twenty-odd years," Mary Lynne told me. "After the triplets were born, I took off seventeen years to raise the kids." No doubt, that birth served as a marker in her life. "I home-schooled them," she said, "until there were six at home and it got to be too much." I had this fleeting picture of all the meals, laundry, and general mayhem that come with having twelve children in one house. Mary Lynne's husband, Patrick, taught Latin and history at Napanee District Secondary School for thirty years, and while he was never directly involved in the dump fight, he always backed his partner.

Mary Lynne returned to teaching in 1995 as a supply teacher. By then the brood of twelve had mostly fled the nest. "I had to choose something worthwhile," she said. "I didn't know where to put my energies." Then she saw an item in the local newspaper, the *Beaver*, about the Richmond Landfill expansion. Steve Medd, a geologist born and bred in Napanee who was soon to be her compatriot in the dump fight, had been quoted. "That's what convinced me," Mary Lynne said. "My background was in geology and geography. I wanted to devote my time to something that was important." Any cause she chose to fight for, I gathered, would concern some abuse of power—Mary Lynne wanted justice for the "little guys."

Throughout the many years of the landfill fight, activist groups formed and reformed, changing their names and membership as citizens fought and burned out before being replaced by others. In 1989, for example, Mary Lynne and a friend formed the Ratepayers Organization of Richmond. Then she joined CARE—Citizens Against the Richmond Expansion. And later, she became active in CCCTE.

In the Ontario election of 1995, Mary Lynne Sammon ran for reeve. That attempt failed. But on another occasion she went before an Ontario Municipal Board hearing to argue against a proposed municipal quarry. These hearings usually find in favour of the developer. But pitted against the proponent's lawyer, Mary Lynne and a fellow activist presented legal arguments—and won. Her face lit up as she told that story.

What Mary Lynne brought to the dump fight was her archivist's touch. She went to the land registry office, the archives of both Lennox and Addington and Hastings counties, and newspaper offices (the *Belleville Intelligencer* and the *Napanee Beaver*) to gather material—so she knew not just the history of the dump but also the history of the area. Her office was piled high with paper and the basement was apparently awash in boxes of documents, all related to the landfill. She talked about "being on a different wavelength"—learning all you can about an issue to enable you and like-minded people to go toe to toe with the other side.

I thought of all the hours that Mary Lynne and I had spent in that land registry office. Odd that historical documents would be housed in newish Service Ontario offices in an industrial mall north of Napanee. The one-storey office features a brown brick facade and a red metal roof, with the Itty Bitty Diner right next door. We marvelled at the huge books in the registry office that had chronicled in pen and ink every sale and purchase of land since the Loyalists first started coming to the area and settling here in the late 1700s.

Mary Lynne learned that the provincial government was going to convert all the records to digital files and then charge a fee for access. The records had always been freely available, with the oldest ones on microfilm; these were readily accessed and could be printed out. Mary Lynne and I worked furiously to get our research done before the records were removed for conversion.

Mary Lynne worked faster than I ever could. She volunteered to put in extra hours to get the job done. We copied deeds and land titles and obtained copies of important reference plans (survey maps). In fact, Mary Lynne put in so many hours when I was not there that I offered to pay her. Besides, she spent a lot on gas commuting from Forest Mills, where she lived. When I paid her, Mary Lynne promptly donated the money to the CCCTE.

I probed a little deeper. I wanted to know what kept Mary Lynne going as the Richmond Landfill fight continued for years and then decades. "I felt a sense," she began, "that it wasn't right to take advantage of people. Many others felt that way. Margaret Walsh, for example, caught on to Waste Management early. We all had this sense of outrage. The company has to provide a service. I understood that. But you don't have to exploit. You don't have to *use* people. The whole thing was an eye opener for me. We were babes in the woods. There was an innocence there."

We talked about what was surely the most memorable public meeting in the whole landfill saga. That was on November 24, 2005, at the Selby Community Hall, just before Waste Management submitted its environmental assessment to the ministry. Steve Medd wanted some answers. He wanted to know how much methane gas would be released into the air if a proposed mega-dump in his municipality went forward. Steve had asked that question six months ago but had not received any answer from the garbage giant. Now he had come to the Selby meeting to ask the question again.

"I want two numbers," he said that night, just minutes into the meeting. "How much gas is leaving the existing site and how much gas would leave the expanded site?"[15] When officials from Waste Management could provide no numbers, chaos erupted. The crowd began to chant and shout.

Mary Lynne smiled as she recalled all this. She was there, of course. "It was wild," she said. "Chief Maracle was there plus the Mohawk warriors." That day in the hospital she talked a lot about the strength of the grass roots. In fact, it was the aspect of the dump fight she was most proud of. "Having people be empowered," she told me. "That's the big thing. Nothing is worse than powerlessness." On that night at Selby, at least, there had been a palpable sense of empowerment.

Waste Management officials could do little to restore order. Allan Gardiner jumped to his feet, and his loud voice boomed out, "O Canada." The crowd stood up and joined him in the national anthem. Company officials seated at the front of the room looked like the proverbial deer in headlights. They looked at each other, confused and unsure of how to respond. They eventually stood up, too, and joined in the singing.

Unable to control his frustration, Ben Sutcliffe—who raised dogs and horses and had endured years of stillborn and deformed pups and foals—bellowed at the top of his voice. He addressed meeting chair Peter Homenuck, a company man, demanding that Waste Management "answer Steve Medd's question!" Ben Sutcliffe refused to be silenced. Pointing a finger at company officials, he shook with rage, almost toppling over. "Steve asked his question six months ago and he still hasn't got any answers," he shouted. "We have to make our living here. We have a few minutes to come up with answers to lies and innuendo . . . You've got one chance—let all of these people know, answer Steve Medd's question! Answer Steve Medd's question!"[16]

The room broke out into a thunderous chant, "*Answer Steve Medd's question! Answer Steve Medd's question!*" Steve Medd himself slid down in his chair, curled up his six-foot-two frame, and put his hands over his head. Sutcliffe dared Homenuck to eject him from the community hall. When the shouting match finally subsided, Waste Management's project engineer, Art Seanor, quietly replied, "I don't have those numbers." Apparently, there was confusion about who was supposed to send out the letter to Steve. Mary Lynne remembered Allan Gardiner's parting comment. "If you don't know who was to send the letter after you've had it written, how does it instill comfort in myself and my fellow neighbours around the landfill that you're running a proper site?" She laughed as she recalled the events of that night.

Mary Lynne then reminded me of that beautiful, sunny day when she and I visited the pioneer cemetery that Janelle Tulloch, a fellow participant in the dump fight, had worked so hard to restore. Hearing that a landfill expansion was planned, Janelle and others who had ancestors buried there became concerned that the site might become a repository for garbage. She went looking and described what time and decades of neglect had done. The site was overgrown with old lilac trees, brambles, and brush. The headstones were covered with moss, cracked, or broken; many had toppled to the ground or were buried under debris. The inscriptions were worn and weathered and in many cases undecipherable. She did, however, identify the last person buried there in 1906. We found the headstone: Wellington Hick, aged 33 years, 9 months, 4 days.

Beginning in the spring of 2001—the lilacs were in bloom—Janelle and her husband, Ken, and a team of volunteers spent many days cleaning up the site and restoring the headstones. Among the finds at the site was a horseshoe, a reminder of a time when the hearse was a horse and wagon. They found the headstone of Ken's ancestors; it had succumbed to over a century and a half of exposure to the weather and elements, and had to be repaired or replaced. We stood at the new headstone: William Tulloch died at age sixty-one on August 26, 1865, and his wife, Margaret, at age fifty-four on August 25, 1865—the deaths were just one day apart. Both were from Stirlingshire, Scotland.

As we walked around, we noticed that the majority of headstones were of marble, but there was an occasional fieldstone, a marker used by poor families—one with the date 1848 inscribed in its centre. Many of those buried here were young children. Mary Lynne noted that in a single year, 1867, the Spencer family buried four children, two sons and two daughters, ranging in age from nine months to six years. Another family buried three one-year-old sons. Doves were commonly engraved on the top portion of a child's headstone. Janelle told us she had identified thirty-six headstones and estimated that forty-nine people were buried here; some family members shared a headstone.

We stopped at the plaque of the Ontario Heritage Trust and Lennox and Addington Historical Society (unveiled on October 8, 2005). Empey Hill Cemetery is protected under the *Ontario Heritage Act*. This meant that although Waste Management owned the land surrounding the cemetery, under the *Ontario Heritage Act*, any plans to change or to develop the property must be approved by the heritage minister, which offered some reassurance for those who worked so diligently for its restoration.

***

Although the fate of the Richmond Landfill was still very much up in the air then (this was January 2015, remember, when the Environmental Review Tribunal hearings had yet to begin), Mary Lynne Sammon could look back on her community service and say with certainty, "I do feel a sense of victory. It's true that the system is cooked but you can beat the system. That's my hope for your book. I hope the book changes attitudes so that people can feel empowered and they don't feel hopeless."

We talked about a former official at Waste Management who had said to a dump opponent, "I have never seen a community fight as hard as this one." Another quote we enjoyed was the one that a journalist procured from a Waste Management official who complained bitterly about being beaten "by a bunch of poor farmers and an old Indian chief." Chief Maracle—who was just over fifty at the time—had objected to being described as old.

Typically, Mary Lynne Sammon did not regret the many, many hours spent going to meetings, writing letters, and standing in protest. "My activism," she said, "was also an education. I liked it. I liked the challenge. It kept me active and alert." She characterized the role that she played as "a persistent presence" and "an unwavering activist." Indeed, among the core group of unwavering activists, Mary Lynne was among the most dogged.

She was grateful, too, that her fellow activists formed relationships with each other. "The people on the committee became good friends," said Mary Lynne. "There was no interference. You could be straight and honest. Nothing was held against me. We liked *you*, Poh-Gek. You helped us. It was fun. If nothing else, we formed friendships."

Mary Lynne talked about activism as a form of consciousness-raising. Implicit was the notion that changing hearts and minds may be invisible and even a little mysterious. "When I first went into politics," Mary Lynne told me, "I was reading Carl Jung. This idea that you can plant a seed and make a difference. You tap into the collective unconscious. It sounds heady, I know."

Mary Lynne was even philosophical about Fred Sutcliffe. In the eyes of some in the community (such as Margaret Walsh, for one), he was the enemy. He had sold out to a corporate landfill company and enriched himself in the process. Mary Lynne didn't see it that way.

"When I went through the records," she said, "we saw he had back taxes owing. It was a matter of survival. He was up against it. No money. I can feel sympathy for him. He was the best garbageman going. His guys took the garbage pails back to the houses."

How remarkable, I thought later. Mary Lynne Sammon didn't bear a grudge against Fred Sutcliffe—for poisoning local land, for endangering the health of his community, for lowering property values and sowing discontent. On the latter count, she was clear-eyed. "In the close-knit community of Selby," Mary Lynne recalled, "you had people stepping out of their roles. They faced ostracism."

Allan Gardiner, who served with Mary Lynne on the CCCTE, warned her—and me—to keep our heads down. Whenever he and I toured lands adjacent to the dump, he would insist that I travel with him in his big white Cadillac. Did he fear local thugs? Disgruntled residents who stood to gain by selling their land to the company? Mary Lynne remembers Allan ("a big man but a gentle soul") telling her, "You never know what some people will do for a hundred dollars."

Just before I left, she said to me, "I am all excited. Just talking about the dump fight invigorated me." It was the last time I saw her.

***

Some months after Mary Lynne died, I talked to some of her fellow activists and sought their impressions of her.

Ian Munro said: "The lasting memory I have of Mary Lynne was her amazing ability to think outside the box. Any time we had a meeting on any dump-related subject, she would offer options (always based on her broad-based knowledge) that often seemed to the rest of us to come out of thin air. More often than not, however, when we discussed her approach it turned out to be a novel and intriguing idea that made us all think about things differently. During the never-ending processes, our group followed a lot of different avenues. Many of those were thanks to Mary Lynne's unique contributions." He also thought that Mary Lynne was a very "aware" person; nothing escaped her attention, especially not the shenanigans of landfill officials.

Marilyn Kendall offered this remembrance: "After a long and contentious public meeting at the high school many years ago, Janelle Tulloch and I, led by Mary Lynne, traipsed across the playing fields in the dark to the fenceline separating the school grounds from the adjacent EnviroPark. The reason? To see what we could discover after recently learning that Waste Management was trucking leachate from the dump and placing it in an underground holding tank before piping it to the sewage treatment plant. We hoped to see the above-ground pumping station (looking for spillage or whatever we could find). Of course, we could see nothing in the dark, but it's an example of how determined we—and especially Mary Lynne—were to investigate all leads."

Mike Bossio was a key figure in the fight when Mary Lynne joined the CCCTE. When asked about Mary Lynne, he wrote this note:

> She understood early on this was going to be a long drawn out battle, and was part of the core team because she had the perseverance necessary to get through the long spells where you just needed to grind away at data—and fundraising. Mary Lynne was so valued by so many because she was one of those unique individuals who came up with brilliant ideas, but more importantly was willing to put in the work necessary to execute those ideas. Everyone has ideas on what should or shouldn't be done, but most people typically want others to execute their ideas. Not Mary Lynne. More than that, she was also willing to do the jobs that no one would take on. She would always be the first to volunteer for whatever needed to be done and never complained about it. She really fit the old adage: if you want to get something done; give it to someone who is busy. She was always busy, and on top of it all, even though she and Patrick had raised twelve kids. Remarkable!
>
> It is hard to even write this because it is so hard to accept that she is gone. Mary Lynne is sorely missed. She was a friend, a comrade in arms, a kindred spirit. Her love for family and community were beyond compare, and I wish she could have been here to see it through to the end. If anyone deserved to see the end of this fight, Mary Lynne is at the top of the list.

CHAPTER 8

A MOUNTAIN OF GARBAGE

"He had not much of a choice. Farmland in the area was difficult to sell because of the dump.... He was getting old and he had no children. Here come the dump guys, and they offer to buy your land. Wouldn't you sell?"
—the response of a neighbour when a farmer sells his land, 1997

As the years turned into decades, some of the older activists pulled back, burned out, or passed away, new players came on the scene, and the name of the citizens' group changed. The Richmond/Tyendinaga Environmental Association would become the Concerned Citizens Committee of Tyendinaga and Environs. Citizens Against the Richmond Expansion was active for many years before merging with the concerned citizens' group in 2005.

Sutcliffe's dumpsite became the Richmond Landfill; Tricil passed it on to Laidlaw, which changed its name to Canadian Waste Services Ltd. and then incorporated. In May 2004, the latter company changed its name to Waste Management of Canada Corporation. Along with the name change, the company adopted a corporate identity similar to its U.S. operations—Waste Management Inc., its parent corporation, is an international company based in Houston, Texas. An aggressive advertising program was launched under the banner "Think Green." Waste Management's vehicles, containers, and uniforms—and even its website—became green.

But people living close to the dump would have been hard pressed to think green when they thought of the dump or any of its managers over the years. More likely residents would connect the dump with the rats that were attracted to the garbage and invaded their homes, along with flies, raccoons, gulls, and other scavenging creatures. Gulls were leaving their droppings everywhere—on the roofs of their houses and cars as well as on vegetables and fruit crops, rendering them inedible. Strong odours emanated from the exposed garbage at the site, and rubbish including garbage bags, cardboard boxes, and loose paper were spread over a wide area within and outside the site as well as along the roadsides. And the numerous garbage trucks, coming and going continuously, exacerbated levels of noise, diesel fumes, and dust.

As the landfill got ever bigger, it became an increasing headache for those in the area. Meetings and more meetings on the issue led to hearings, tribunals, and court cases—with Richard Lindgren of the Canadian Environmental Law Association leading the citizens and their allies over the course of seventeen years. The battles were endless—over the terms of reference, over environmental assessments and technical reports. Nothing about this issue, not even the closing of the dump when that came to pass, would be smooth and easy.

Provincial courts weighed in on the Richmond Landfill saga. On August 25, 2004, the Ontario Court of Appeal had set aside an earlier ruling by the Ontario Divisional Court, which had quashed the terms of reference of the environmental assessment for the proposed landfill expansion. "The judgement raises the fundamental issue of whether courts should defer to ministerial decisions on questions of statutory interpretation," said Richard Lindgren. Patrick Schindler, the lawyer for the Mohawks, said, "The case raises the question whether the fiduciary duty which ministers of the Crown owe to First Nations includes a duty to take into consideration the concerns of the First Nation about a large garbage dump which may adversely impact their territory."[17] The Supreme Court's decision, which came down early in March 2005, refused to grant leave to appeal. It was a big disappointment to CCCTE and the Mohawks of the Bay of Quinte, who had submitted the applications, but they took comfort in the court's decision to award costs to Canadian Waste Services (now Waste Management). Lindgren used the analogy of a boxing match to describe the ongoing process. "That was the end of Round I, but there's like fourteen more rounds to go," he said. "That's the end of the line as far as that appeal is concerned."[18]

The citizens fought tooth and nail against the dump and endless plans to expand the site, and just when they thought they had won, the company turned around and said, *Let's build a new dump—right beside the old one.* The geology next door, of course, was the same fractured limestone that made the first site such a poor choice for a mega-dump. The minister of the environment had rejected a mega-expansion in 2006 on the grounds that the geology was unsuitable and unsafe for garbage disposal. Right after that, a new minister approved the terms of reference for a second proposed expansion with the same geology. The citizens were puzzled and shocked. *This decision made no sense*, some said. *What was the ministry thinking?*

More years went by, and the mountain of garbage grew right along with the boxes of documents lugged to this or that hearing by lawyers on either side of the issue. The leachate plume got longer and bigger, but by continuing to buy up land around the landfill site, the company could truthfully say that no contaminants were leaving its property.

***

The mountain of garbage literally stank to high heaven. One evening in 2004, Howard O'Connor spoke to Greater Napanee town council. The long-time resident, then in his nineties, had been a flight sergeant with the Royal Air Force's Bomber Command and had received the Distinguished Flying Medal from King George VI at Buckingham Palace. I was curious about the award. He explained that it was for a small adventure he had back in 1943. After a bombing run over Germany, his four-engine Stirling bomber was attacked by three German night-fighters that knocked out two of his engines, putting the plane into a nosedive. He managed to pull out of the dive and used the stars for direction to steer him and seven members of his crew safely back to an airbase in Britain. He added, sadly, that only two of the seven recruits from Napanee returned home safely.

During this particular phase of the dump fight, at issue was a proposal for a massively expanded dump that would accept some 750,000 tonnes of garbage a year. Sutcliffe's original little dump, remember, accepted 15,000 tonnes. A Dinky toy compared to the monster truck that was now on the table.

That night in Napanee, Howard O'Connor offered his perspective on the expansion. "I find it difficult to comprehend the vastness of this proposal for the site," he said. "We have a mountain of garbage at the present site . . . and less than one percent of garbage comes from Napanee." O'Connor said he saw the town a little differently from most people. "I view this town from the air. I have this hobby and fly an aircraft . . . over this beautiful town—the Napanee River, Bay of Quinte, Lake Ontario, the forests and farmlands."

His flights also took him over the current landfill site. "The smell of that seeps into the cockpit of the aircraft and you can't breathe," he said. "Then I see the water running off that mountain into the streams and the Salmon River. I believe we should have a referendum . . . as soon as possible."

O'Connor stressed to council that he was not speaking on behalf of any organization or group. "I've lived here all my life, and I'll be damned if I want to see this town be destroyed by a landfill like that."[19] Howard O'Connor died in the fall of 2013; he had been up in his plane just the week before. He never did get the referendum he was seeking.

***

As time marched on and citizen activists found their lives consumed by the dump issue, two hard facts became obvious. First, the provincial

Ministry of the Environment had neither the staff nor the will to do battle with industry. The bureaucrats, most of them, saw their task as facilitators. Second, citizens came to understand that taking on a multinational waste company consumed not only time but also money. Pots of it, and more than any of them ever had.

Expert witnesses had to be paid and their travel and accommodation costs looked after. Activists travelled to Toronto to meet with politicians and bureaucrats, so money was needed for food, gas, and hotel rooms. The hat was passed and residents dug into their own savings. A resident was heard to remark, "It's like taking food off our tables." But mostly money was raised the old-fashioned way—garage sales, bake sales, and raffles. Fundraising was a constant worry. Somehow, they managed to raise some $250,000 over the course of the fight, so they could at least stay in the game and compete with companies that had no shortage of paid staff and expert witnesses at their disposal.

From 1988 to 1996 in Ontario, funds were made available ahead of proceedings to community groups and individuals concerned about the environmental impacts of developments—such as landfill and quarry proposals. Intervenor funding, as it was called, owed its beginnings to Thomas Berger and the Berger Commission of the 1970s. Berger, a judge in British Columbia, headed the royal commission looking at the proposed Mackenzie Valley Pipeline. Justice Berger solicited testimony about the social, environmental, and economic impacts of the pipeline, as well as the opinions of anyone who was affected by the project. Recognizing that many members of the public could not access the financial resources to have their interests represented at the hearings, he concluded that funding was necessary to ensure their participation.

"These groups are sometimes called public interest groups," Berger said at the time, "because they represent interests that the public believes ought to be considered before a decision is made. They represent identifiable interests that should not be ignored, that indeed it is essential should be heard. They do not represent the public interest, but it is in the public interest that they should participate in the Inquiry."[20] Berger explained, "The pipeline companies will not take it amiss if I say that I do not want to rely upon them to represent the environment totally."[21]

A dozen environmental groups in the Northwest Territories wished to take part in the Berger Inquiry, as did other parties. The federal government provided funding to allow this to happen. The initiative represented the first intervenor funding program in the history of Canadian environmental hearings. In time, a similar model came to be deployed in Ontario.

Ian G. Scott, who had been counsel for the Berger Commission, was appointed Ontario's attorney general in 1985. He instituted intervenor funding based on the model adopted in the Berger Inquiry, but with one important difference: funding came not from the government but from proponents. The "Ontario model," as some called it, was lauded by the international community, and continued to be in force until Premier Mike Harris came into power in 1995 with an overwhelming Progressive Conservative majority. This government, elected on the platform of the so-called Common Sense Revolution, started to dismantle environmental legislation and to amend regulations, including intervenor funding.

On March 28, 1996, a notice quietly appeared on the *Environmental Bill of Rights* (EBR) Registry, a government website that includes public notices about environmental issues, with the title "Sunsetting of *The Intervenor Funding Project Act.*"[22] The government gave notice of a decision "to permit the Act to sunset [expire] as originally intended. This decision is consistent with our commitment to make hearings more efficient and to reduce non-essential administrative processes." Brenda Elliott, minister of the environment and energy, called the step "part of our new approach to improving environmental decision-making."[23]

The Waste Management Association, a lobby group for the waste industry, lauded the government's decision. The Act had been criticized by the industry for requiring increased expense and time for environmental hearings.

Environmental advocates, on the other hand, vehemently opposed the government's decision. Letting the legislation die, they said, would give companies and governments the upper hand in dealing with those who opposed projects with potential adverse impacts. The government pointed out that in hearings before the Environmental Assessment Board, the Ontario Energy Board, and the Joint Board, participants would still continue to be eligible for cost awards *at the end* of the hearings, stressing that it would continue to encourage proponents to provide participant funding on a voluntary basis. Minister Elliott subscribed to the view that citizens affected by projects would be able to influence assessments effectively without intervenor funding. It would be in the interests of those proposing developments, she said, to consult with the public, because consultation requirements were contained in environmental assessment legislation. "People are able to come forward as *volunteers* still."[24]

James Bradley, the Liberal environment minister from 1985 to 1990, spoke strongly in defence of keeping intervenor funding:

The big companies, the major corporations, can afford the best lawyers and they can afford the so-called scientific and technical experts. So you're quite content in this government to have the most powerful people and the richest people have their say at a hearing, but you're very reluctant to have those who aren't powerful and those who don't have the money have their say. That's what intervenor funding did. You wanted those people to go out and have the bake sales and sell raffle tickets and so on. I can tell you that any of the major companies in this province didn't have to have a raffle to hire the best lawyers in the province. They always had the high-priced . . . they had the best lawyers in the province, the best experts in the province and they used to run roughshod over anybody who was opposed to what they wanted.[25]

***

Another issue was unfolding at the same time that intervenor funding was drying up. The Harris government brought in an extensive program of municipal amalgamation. Opposition was widespread and acrimonious because residents felt that larger amalgamated municipalities would destroy their way of life and sense of community. The restructuring program from 1996 to 2001 reduced the number of municipalities in Ontario from 850 to 444.[26]

On January 1, 1998, residents in southwestern Lennox and Addington County woke up to find that five familiar municipalities—Napanee, Richmond, North Fredericksburgh, South Fredericksburgh, and Adolphustown—had disappeared. The amalgamation of these municipalities brought into existence the Town of Greater Napanee, with a collective population of 14,500. The building where Sir John A. Macdonald gave his last campaign speech in 1891 became the administrative centre.

The province had argued that fiscal savings would accrue by eliminating duplicated services in municipalities close to one another while reducing the number of municipal officials and bureaucrats. In reality, the Town of Greater Napanee experienced the opposite, as did many other amalgamated municipalities. The total number of elected officials was reduced from twenty-five to seven, but the cost savings were minimal. The pay for these offices had essentially been analogous to honorariums. And increased funding responsibilities, especially for welfare, social housing, and ambulances, had to be taken over by the municipalities.

Kelley Hineman, warden of Lennox and Addington during the restructuring of the county, told me, "The only cost savings was for the province.

The municipal expense tripled when you added in the downloading of services. The whole thing was smoke and mirrors so the province could lighten its economic output to municipalities."

For the citizens of Richmond Township, the folding of their municipality into the Town of Greater Napanee had serious implications for their relationship with and opposition to the Richmond Landfill. The former municipalities all became wards after amalgamation. The council of the new town was made up of a mayor and a deputy mayor, both elected at large, and a councillor from each ward. Richmond Township was now a ward that was represented by one councillor on the town council; this councillor did not have to live or own property in the ward.

In the former Richmond, there had been a council of five—reeve, deputy reeve, and three councillors—all of whom had to live in the township or own property there. Council members had thus had first-hand knowledge of living near a landfill and mostly supported the opposition efforts of the citizens who were their neighbours. Councillors of the new town were now more distant figures who neither fully understood nor fully appreciated the effects of the landfill on quality of life in the area. Their support could not be counted upon, as their concerns appeared to be mainly economic—and more urban than rural.

Similarly, many residents in the new Town of Greater Napanee had no personal experience of living in proximity to a landfill. They were unlikely to support opposition to the convenience of garbage disposal. The residents of the former Richmond Township remembered community events such as celebration of Richmond Day and community pig-roasts. That kind of small community identification was now a thing of the past.

So a kind of perfect storm was at work as citizens fought against the landfill expansion. The funding that had been available for such fights was no longer available, and whatever political control little Richmond Township had to determine its own fate was lost.

The pitched and prolonged battle between a few dozen diehard environmentalists in a tiny community in southeastern Ontario and a series of corporate landfill owners should have been no contest. The citizens had no money, other than what they could raise themselves. The other side was awash in financial and political clout. They should have run roughshod over the local residents—and they certainly tried. But they weren't able to. That's why I find this story so compelling.

CHAPTER 9

KING RICHARD

"It's time for everybody in this room, all the local municipalities, the Mohawks, other interested parties, and most importantly, the minister of the environment . . . to stand up and just say no to this expansion. It's a bad idea, at the wrong site, at the wrong time, and for the wrong reasons."
—Richard Lindgren, staff lawyer with the Canadian
Environmental Law Association, 2006

This day is what Richard Lindgren calls "a battery recharging day." The fifty-five-year-old environmental lawyer, a tireless advocate who seems not to sleep much, has been working on the Richmond dump file since 1999—when he was thirty-nine. Every member of the citizens' group opposing the mega-dump has stories to tell of emails arriving from Rick in the small hours, or of a huge document adroitly assessed and summed up in short order. *How did he do that?* is a common question.

In the wake of a raucous public meeting or a day-long hearing, I would sometimes join Rick at a nearby pub with activists and another expert witness—often hydrogeologist Wilf Ruland—and the grin never left Rick's face. They drank microbrewery beer, while I would shock the server by ordering milk. Smart, funny, a little cocky, and a born storyteller, Rick has the bearing of a player-coach, adept both on the field and behind the scenes, plotting strategy and next moves. He was one of us, yet not. His calm was reassuring. *The odds are stacked against us, and the game is rigged,* I took him to say, *but hey, we can win this thing.*

This day offers another clue to the man's makeup. When Rick works, he works—like a sled dog in harness, always pulling. But when he plays, he knows how to put his feet up. Today he is at his most relaxed and doing the thing he loves most. "We're going fishing," he told me, and we arranged to meet at what he called "the day docks" by a waterfront Kingston hotel.

His twenty-one-foot boat is called *Lady Hawk.* "That's what it was called when I bought it," he says, "and it's bad luck to change it." The boat is pitching in the high winds and waves off Fort Henry on a warm mid-September day in 2015. A few weeks earlier, Rick had sent me photos of two monster fish he had caught in these waters that summer. One was

"The fight to stop the Richmond Landfill is 'winnable.'" Environmental lawyer Rick Lindgren speaks to local citizens for the first time on December 8, 1999, at a Marysville parish hall. Photo courtesy of the *Napanee Beaver.*

a twenty-five-pound salmon. Rick's smile as he held it was almost as wide as the fish itself.

Today he's wearing a ball cap with the Team Canada logo (the white cutout of a hockey player set against a red and black maple leaf)—a nod to his love for that game. He plays old-timer hockey year-round and has no thoughts of quitting, despite sustaining multiple fractures to his leg years ago by crashing into the boards; he was sidelined for months learning to walk again. His T-shirt makes mention of a sailfish, and I wondered if it was a souvenir of a time spent angling on the ocean.

"Nope," Rick said. "Bought it at The Bay." He described an occasion when he and his wife, Laura Lee, were vacationing in the Cayman Islands. "I wanted to catch a marlin," he said. "I wanted to be like that character in *The Old Man and the Sea.*" But the outfitters wanted a thousand dollars to take them out onto the ocean. He declined.

Rick is one of five lawyers who work for the Canadian Environmental Law Association. He calls himself "a public interest lawyer earning a public interest salary." Just as Legal Aid is a publicly funded law service for individuals who cannot afford legal representation, CELA (which is funded by Legal Aid Ontario) offers legal help to community groups fighting unwanted development that may pose a threat to the environment.

Rick Lindgren came to the landfill battle by a somewhat circuitous route. At her Richmond Township office one day in April 1999, Reeve

Margaret Walsh heard an announcement on the local radio that Paul Muldoon, an environmental lawyer from CELA, was speaking in Peterborough. Unable to be there because of previous commitments, she asked Steve Geneja to attend and to get information on obtaining legal assistance. Geneja was deputy land registrar for Hastings County, and an active member and first chair of the citizens' group opposing the landfill expansion. Fourteen years old in 1943, he had lied about his age, joined the navy, and gone to sea in the North Atlantic on convoy duty, returning home to purchase a farm of a hundred acres on Blessington Road for sixteen thousand dollars under the *Veterans' Land Act.*

Geneja attended Muldoon's talk and afterwards approached him about the problem residents were having with the landfill expansion. This was the pivotal encounter that led to the citizens' group obtaining Lindgren's services.

Rick describes the Richmond Landfill saga as the longest-running case that CELA has ever handled. There are, he notes, several aspects that set it apart. Foremost is the multiplicity of impacts of the dump on the air and water, the odours and rats and flies, the noise of the trucks, the impact on property values—and the leachate. "We've had cases of leachate in the past," Rick says, "but this one is *so* apparent and *so* uncontested." In addition, and this is an impact I had not considered, many worthy community groups elsewhere in the province have been denied representation owing to the extended "trench warfare" being fought against Waste Management.

"The hard reality," Rick says, "is that there are a lot of good cases that we can't take because we're tied up with this fight." He was co-counsel with CELA on the Walkerton Inquiry on that community's tainted water tragedy back in 2002, a case that likewise gummed up the works for several years. Meanwhile, there is no pressure from CELA on Rick to wrap up this case or throw in the towel. "We're in for a penny," he says. "We're in for a pound."

***

I didn't have a fishing licence, so I was more deckhand than fisher this morning. Rick had set two fishing rods into handles at the back of the boat so he could troll two lines at the same time. I took the wheel and tried to keep the prow of the boat heading towards a point of land that Captain Lindgren had declared (a lighthouse, a ferry dock). What should have been an easy task was not—I was hard to port then hard to starboard; I over-steered and over-corrected, over-steered and over-corrected as the *Lady Hawk* carved a lazy S pattern through the waters off Point Frederick and Wolfe Island.

Rick seemed not to mind that he was catching nothing. The few times a rod bent, on reeling it in it produced only green plants from the lake bottom.

"What's the appeal of fishing?" I asked him.

Turns out it's not a sport. It's a philosophy.

"It's not about catching fish," he told me. "It's about being out on the water. There are many who live in Kingston who have never been out on the water. They've never taken the Wolfe Island ferry at night to see the city from the water. They're really missing out. Time spent fishing doesn't count against you when the great reckoning comes. And some of my best days on the water end with me having nothing to show for it."

Rick has—much to his wife's chagrin, as he puts it—twenty fishing rods and a fifty-pound tackle box. When he opened it up to change lures, trays within trays revealed a dazzling array of hooks, leaders, and sinkers and all manner of fishing paraphernalia. Rick likes trolling because only the bigger, aggressive fish will attack bait or lures on the move, and that means dinner, sometimes many dinners.

Rick grew up in Kingston. His father was an avid fisher who passed on that passion to his son. Rick remembered one summer as a law student working as "a special supernumerary constable" on a Royal Canadian Mounted Police boat patrolling the waters off Kingston, and checking to see if boaters had proper registration and life jackets. "Best summer job I ever had," he said.

Rick studied history at Queen's University and then went into law school thinking he might specialize in family law. But in his second year, he took the only available course on environmental law and heard lectures from two CELA lawyers. "A light bulb went off," is how he put it. After graduating, he sent in one application letter—to CELA. He was hired in 1986 and never left.

He joked with me that he's on the Freedom 95 plan. No cushy or early retirement for him. "I can see myself doing this in ten years," he said. "I'm just as charged up now as I was fifteen years ago."

***

After two hours of fruitless trolling ("We'll go out again," he promised; "next time I *guarantee* a fish"), we pulled into the docks at Cedar Island, which affords a stunning view of Fort Henry. The fort was built in the early 1800s in anticipation of an American invasion that never did materialize. At least not yet.

Rick and I tied up the boat and sought the shade at a picnic table. The island is actually a national park and its few campsites are much sought after in high summer. He offered me some banana bread, bought at the

Wolfe Island general store in Marysville—not two minutes from Rick's house. Rick and his wife, Laura Lee, have lived on the island (where she was raised) for twenty-three years. He thought living in Toronto was okay, but its "concrete canyons" left him feeling disconnected from the elements. The young parents concluded that the island would be the best place to raise their two daughters, Anna and Rachel. One of them is now finishing a journalism degree; the other is studying law with a possible focus on social justice and immigration issues.

Wolfe Island was much in the news several years ago when eighty-six wind turbines were installed on the island, dividing the community between those who welcomed the income from having one on their property and those who opposed them on the grounds that they were harmful to health and property values. "There's no science showing medical impacts from wind turbines," Rick said, and all attempts by taxpayers to have their taxes lowered on the grounds that the turbines lowered their property values have failed.

For many years, Rick taught courses in environmental law at Queen's. He would take his boat across the lake, fishing along the way and again on the way home. For a passionate angler, commuting doesn't get any better than that.

What Rick gains from a long-running case such as the Waste Management fight is an ongoing education in hydrogeology, wetland ecology, and technical and scientific evidence. That is part of the appeal of battling against unwanted and environmentally reckless development such as a mega-dump. "I love the work," he told me. "The Richmond Landfill case has been a good case, with every aspect of environmental law involved, with side trips to the courts, the Environmental Review Tribunal, all the educational approaches."

And for Rick, the fight is personal. "I like the water," he said. "And when someone wants to install a facility that puts that water at risk, it gets my blood boiling."

The Environmental Review Tribunal held a public hearing in spring 2015 at locations in Belleville and Tyendinaga Township. Rick would give me a ride to the hearing each morning. From the window of my home I could see the ferry making its way from Wolfe Island to Kingston. When it approached the ferry dock, I'd run down to the street to meet him. The ride to the hearing was a time to discuss issues relevant to that day's proceedings. At the venue, I would watch Rick haul his cases of documents into the hearing room. He would set up shop at a desk on the left side of the room, with the Mohawks' lawyer, Eric Gillespie, and his assistant, Priya Vittal, lined up behind him. Chief Don Maracle was almost always there as well. On the other side of the room were the Waste Management lawyer and his three-person legal team, along with the Ontario Ministry of the Environment's legal team. I noticed the greater number of bodies on the other side of the room. The folks over there seemed to be wearing flashier suits than those on our side. It would be easy to conclude that the lone CELA lawyer was outgunned.

But not so. The tribunal's chair (by convention referred to as "the ERT member"), Maureen Carter-Whitney, was to issue her findings near the end of 2015. The conditions she set down for the closure of the dump could well mean the end of the battle, with a much-hoped-for victory for the citizens' side. They had reason for cautious optimism—an interim order she had issued in July 2015 had set more stringent conditions for monitoring the landfill site.

"What a group," Rick said of the concerned citizens' committee. "They never get tired. Sadly, a few have died without seeing the end of this fight. Usually in these fights, especially when the case drags on as this one has, people get burned out. These people have remained active and so effective for so long."

Like many observers in this environmental battle, Rick laments that the provincial ministries of natural resources and the environment no longer have the ability to properly perform their watchdog function. "Many have said this," explained Rick. "Both the Ministry of Natural Resources and the Ministry of the Environment have been crippled by budget cuts. They don't have the institutional capacity to do the job. The Ministry of the Environment [and Climate Change, its new moniker] especially is a shell of its former self. It's under-resourced and understaffed."

Compounding that issue is that the whole environmental assessment process needs an overhaul, but there's no political will to do that. Rick Lindgren was part of a ministry-appointed panel of experts that met in 2004–2005 to look at how assessments are handled, but their forty-one recommendations were never implemented. One of the most pressing issues is the matter of intervenor funding, which expired under former Ontario premier Mike Harris in 1996. Two years ago, when Rick and another CELA lawyer approached the minister of the environment about the need for reform, they were politely told there was no need.

"I'm livid," Rick said. "The environmental commissioner is livid. People are caught between a rock and a hard place. The loss of funding is a significant rollback. But I see no signals that this government wants to improve environmental assessments. The process is fundamentally flawed."

***

Has the battle been won against Waste Management? It's still too early to tell. Rick said he would only celebrate victory when either the company withdraws its application to develop the latest reincarnation of a dumpsite—the Beechwood Road Environmental Centre—or the minister turns the application down. If the minister does that, it would mark the second time an Ontario minister of the environment has turned down an application on this same site. Rick and the citizens he represents have celebrated in the past what they took to be a victory, only to be tossed back into the fray, "with BREC rising from the ashes. People were dumbfounded."

Rick had never seen a landfill expansion stay alive after the Ministry of the Environment had rejected it—and he had never seen a rejection so strongly worded. "Yet here we are," he told me. "Never say never."

Rick is a veteran of these wars, and community activists would do well to heed his advice. Here's his counsel.

Get organized. "Make links. There is strength in numbers. Reach out to friends and neighbours. We would have had no chance without the involvement and co-operation of the Mohawks of the Bay of Quinte. That's the only reason we were successful during the first environmental assessment process."

Pick your spots. "Early on, I kept stressing to the citizens' group, 'Don't fight everything or you'll get burnout.' We focus on issues with the biggest bang for the buck."

Get going on fundraising. "You'll need a lawyer. CELA is free, but if you can't get CELA you'll have to hire a lawyer. But lawyers are not magicians. You also need good experts. With concerned citizens of Napanee, what really stands out is their creativity in fundraising."

Rick has, of course, moved on to fight other fights in other communities but he keeps a close eye on the landfill file. But the Richmond Landfill fight is one that weighs on him—simply because of all the documentation, all the years spent, all the friends made. He still thought of the Richmond Landfill as the worst dumpsite in Ontario, and held out hope that the ERT member would put another nail—maybe the final nail—in that coffin.

CHAPTER 10

LEARNING THE ROPES AND RAISING A STINK

"If residents living near the Richmond Landfill think the odours are bad now, they haven't smelled anything yet."
—Wilf Ruland, hydrogeologist and expert witness for the *no* side, 2003

For almost a decade, drivers heading west on Highway 401 near Napanee would have spotted a yellow school bus conspicuously parked in a field on the north side of the road. At its rear was a large white board with a classic red Stop sign and beside it in black, "Richmond Landfill Expansion" and, in smaller print, "Protect Our Water and Farmlands." The sign was on the property of Allan Gardiner, whose farmland abutted the highway.

The protest sign was prompted by Allan's anger and frustration. It first appeared in the summer of 1999. He had been attending the public consultation meetings organized by Canadian Waste Services for the terms of reference of the environmental assessment. These sessions had been going on for more than a year, with the company presenting information on everything from the use of contaminated soil for daily cover of waste to loss of property values, from nuisance seagulls to noisy truck traffic. It became increasingly clear to Allan that the so-called consultations were a sham—"smoke and mirrors," as he once put it.

The community was seeking reassurance about the safety of its water and air, and other issues related to its environment and quality of life. Canadian Waste Services, in sharp contrast, was focused entirely on achieving an expanded landfill site. The two sides' discourse took place on different planes. Committee members and residents grew weary of the two-hour evening meetings. During the last public consultation meeting on June 17, 1999, Allan Gardiner bluntly stated, "I am attending under duress. After participating in these meetings since February 1998, I am fed up." Few area residents disagreed with his position.

The school bus protest sign went up on his property soon after that. It was only removed, and the bus driven away, sometime in 2007 when the mega-dump expansion was defeated and the snow had melted. Allan mentioned to me that he used the old school bus for storing his farm tools and

Protest yellow school bus on Allan Gardiner's farmland adjacent
to Highway 401. Photo courtesy of Steve Medd.

he could bring it back anytime it was needed. But he hoped that he would
never need it again.

What especially irked Allan was the excessive amount of technical jargon contained in company documents and meeting agendas. Tactic number one for the developer seemed to be to drown the opposition in paper and bafflegab. Residents attending the meetings were overwhelmed by the presentations, especially with the details and data. Farmers and small-town residents were pitted against seasoned professional consultants. One resident noted that the terms of reference needed to be presented in everyday terms—"You shouldn't need a lawyer to understand it."

With consultants making no apparent effort to communicate with them at an appropriate level, citizens were unable to assess whether the information was valid or accurate. Neither were they able to evaluate potential environmental and health impacts. Residents began to feel uneasy about two things: the company repeatedly minimizing the negative aspects of the proposed expansion, and its many assurances that potential impacts—the company conceded there were some—could be mitigated.

Allan and his neighbours were intelligent people, and some of them were well educated, but none had the experience or even the vocabulary. Terms of reference—on first encountering the term, they asked: *What's that?* Environmental assessment? Leachate plume, overburden, hydrogeology, odour incident, liner integrity . . .

A crash course was underway in landfill lingo. Some of the people around Napanee in those days understood the terms, but virtually all of them worked for the company, and they weren't exactly sharing. The waters, metaphorical and real, were being muddied.

***

When I think of Allan Gardiner, I think of his outrage at seeing the land, water, and air of his community so sullied. He was heartbroken when the hard maples in the swamp died—he had taken me to the site one fall day to see the spectacular foliage of the "swamp maples." And the odours from the landfill—at times they were severe enough to invade homes. One resident complained that he could never plan a barbecue because the smell could be so offensive.

Allan recounted an incident regarding a neighbour who lived adjacent to the landfill. "I was standing outside his house talking to him," he told me. "The odour of rotting garbage was so bad that I asked him, 'How can you stand the smell?' He said, 'What smell?'" Allan was convinced that the man's "smelling apparatus" had been damaged.

Suspecting that Allan may have got it right, I went looking for a scientific basis for loss of smell. I found data showing that olfactory (smell) receptors are in a relatively unprotected position, and are susceptible to damage from pollutants in the ambient air leading to decreased smell function. This factor may, in fact, play a role in age-related smell loss. Further, since taste is closely linked to smell, it may also lead to loss of taste. These health effects of noxious landfill odours have largely been ignored.

During Allan's long involvement in the dump battle, his anger boiled over many times. During one of many demonstrations, the citizens took a petition to city hall. "The terms of reference were flawed," yelled Allan Gardiner. "You didn't listen to us."

Council members tabled the petition for later discussion without comment.

***

By 2001, there was a new mayor in Greater Napanee—David Remington. On January 11 of that year, he called a news conference (open to media only) to release a progress report of an audit done by Terraprobe, an environmental engineering firm, on the hydrogeology of the existing landfill. Anti-dump protesters had crashed the event and erupted in anger when Remington announced that the town dump was not leaking contaminants. "Groundwater contaminant pathways are controlled, and no significant movements of leachate were detected," he maintained. "We are satisfied with the results so far. The additional wells and increased water

Demonstration protesting the Richmond Landfill
expansion (January 12, 2005). Photo courtesy of the
Napanee Beaver.

sampling ensure better monitoring."[27] The landfill site was not affecting the water in neighbouring properties, and it appeared to be well maintained, Remington said.

"These people are buying bottled water because they're afraid to drink from their own wells," shouted a livid Allan Gardiner. "Don't tell us the dump isn't leaking!"[28] Known for his explosive temper, Allan had to be restrained by his son Iain. Remington could not continue, and he and the hired engineer left through a back door as residents continued to vent their anger at town staff.

There were more and more meetings, and more and more insults. Insults to the local environment, and to the intelligence of local people. At a workshop at Selby Community Hall in early January 2002, Canadian Waste Services talked about leachate treatment. One option, the company said, was to discharge treated leachate into Marysville Creek, the Salmon River, and the Bay of Quinte. It did not provide details on how the leachate was going to be treated. If the landfill expansion were approved, the company estimated that approximately 100,000 gallons (380,000 litres) of leachate would have to be siphoned off from the site each day.

The disclosure shocked people at the workshop, including Allan Gardiner. "It was a farce tonight," he said after the meeting. One resident had asked a very good question: If the treated leachate is safe, why not send it directly to the Greater Napanee Water Treatment Plant and into the town's drinking water system? Company officials said regulations would prevent such a move. Allan seized on the point as he exited the meeting. "They said it wasn't pure enough. If it's not pure enough to go into the water treatment plant, why would you put it into the Salmon River?"

I don't want to create the impression that Allan Gardiner was always angry with the landfill company. There were times when he praised them if he thought they had responded well. But inevitably, some new development would cause him to lose trust and his anger would flare anew. When Allan died in 2013, his obituary in the *Napanee Beaver* mentioned his political past—former warden, former deputy reeve, his activism in the Ontario Federation of Agriculture, his life spent farming, and how his "big smile and bigger personality will be sorely missed." But there was also this: "He was a tireless advocate for protecting our local environment through his passionate involvement to oppose the Richmond Dump expansion."[29]

***

Allan would talk of the smells that emanated from the dump, smells that sometimes made him nauseous. For some reason, he said, it was especially bad on Sundays. One of his neighbours, fellow farmer Doug Cranston, complained that the smell bore strong traces of tobacco and burned rubber. He thought his cows had gotten sick and breathless from breathing the bad air and drinking the bad water, and they suffered from diarrhea. Tests showed that both Allan's well and that of his neighbour were contaminant-free, but neither of them trusted that water. Their families stuck to bottled water. Later, tests revealed that the Cranstons' well was contaminated. There's no way of knowing whether that contamination was new or had been undetected earlier.

The smells emanating from the dump were a major headache for anyone with the misfortune to live nearby or downwind. In 2003, the concerned citizens' committee hired hydrogeologist Wilf Ruland, who, like lawyer Rick Lindgren, had a lot of experience with landfills. One of their issues, Wilf underlined, was smell.

In fall 2002, Napanee mayor David Remington had heard about a new addition to the expansion proposal: an excavation plan that "kind of came out of left field," as he put it to Seth DuChene of the *Napanee Beaver*. Should the dump expansion win provincial approval, old garbage in the dump would be moved from an old unlined section to a newer lined section. At the time, it didn't seem like a bad idea to the mayor. Opponents of the landfill expansion had long expressed concerns about the impact on groundwater and surface water of leachate from the oldest unlined section of the dump.

But Remington was disabused of his notions when Wilf Ruland came to the council's regular meeting on March 10, 2003, to deliver a disturbing message. "If residents living near the Richmond Landfill think the odours are bad now near the dump," he said, "they haven't smelled anything yet."[30]

While some of the decaying garbage removed would be relocated to a new lined section of the landfill, some would be used as cover material. The process would occur over a period of about ten years between April and November of each year. Ruland, who had studied landfills and their impacts for fifteen years, said he had been present at landfills when minor excavations were taking place, and the odours were "awful and unbearable."

And those excavations had not approached the scale that Canadian Waste Services was proposing. The plan was unlike anything that Ruland had ever seen attempted in Canada. "This is not something a good corporate neighbour would do," he said. Asked by one councillor how a company could reasonably have its employees at the landfill work under those conditions, Ruland said he had no idea how any worker could bear the stench for any length of time, let alone all day, every day.

Ruland pointed out that the proposal to excavate the entire existing Richmond Landfill had been sprung on the community. There was no mention of this proposal in the terms of reference or in the material presented by the proponent and its consultants. The proposed excavation had suddenly surfaced. Ruland did not understand the rationale for "this bizarre scheme," and no explanation was provided. He speculated that the main motivations may have been to enable Canadian Waste Services to landfill to the proposed forty-metre height throughout the existing landfill area and to salvage cover soils from the existing landfill to help ease an anticipated shortage.[31]

Ruland predicted that properties nearest the landfill would be almost unlivable for at least a decade. Residents, Ruland advised, needed to make it clear that the waste excavation was absolutely unacceptable and that the company should drop its plans.

In mid-March 2003, Penny Stewart and Andrew Morley, officials from the Ministry of the Environment, were making their way to Empey Hill church to attend an evening environmental assessment meeting when they noticed a very strong and objectionable odour. Allan Gardiner, who met them outside the church, said, "I thought Penny was going to throw up." As the meeting progressed, the odours invaded the church hall basement. People there asked landfill manager Michael Walters what chemicals they were being exposed to. Walters said he had no specific data on the gas. Morley confirmed that the ministry had received 162 complaints of odour emissions between January 1, 2002, and March 21, 2003.

Stewart served Canadian Waste Services with an order to provide a written action plan within seven days to address ongoing odour complaints. Residents pointed out that they had been lodging complaints for more than a year, but the ministry only acted when its own officials experienced the smell. The company, residents said, cannot manage odours at the dump now. How would it manage a dump six times bigger?

***

The years marched on, more and more meetings were held, and the subject of smell—like the odours themselves—did not subside. In a meeting at the Strathcona Paper Centre in 2006, Wilf Ruland told a gathering of some two hundred people that after examining a number of landfill assessments, waste management master plans, and siting proposals, he regarded the Richmond Landfill expansion proposal as "probably the worst of the bunch." "To my mind, this application is incomplete, there are key pieces that just aren't there," he said. "This includes how they are going to treat the leachate? How they are going to monitor the site? What are they going to do if something goes wrong with their contingency plan and some of the baseline monitoring analysis?"[32]

Ruland regarded the reclamation plan as "wrongheaded" and "inappropriate." "There is about 3 million tonnes of waste at the Richmond site, so it's in between a medium and big sized landfill already, on the scale of landfills in the province. For the proposal, to entirely dig up that whole hill of garbage, and try to screen out the soil materials and re-landfill the waste, it's offensive to me as a professional." The odours released through the proposed ten-year excavation process would be appalling. "I would be very, very disappointed in the province if they ever got approval. I can't see that happening, and on that ground alone, I think the ministry has no choice right now but to reject this environmental assessment."[33]

In his analysis of surface water and groundwater, Ruland identified leachate treatment as a huge problem in the application. Ruland believed there was no such thing as a leak-proof landfill. While more than 90 per cent and even as much as 99 per cent was going to be contained, where was the remaining leachate going to go?

Kevin Murphy, a local farmer, said he farmed about a kilometre down from a leachate discharge location, and pointed to seasonal flooding as his concern. "If you drive by there in the spring, all the farm fields flood. There are 300 to 400 acres of farmland that it floods across. What happens to that land?" Ruland added that Waste Management was proposing to discharge leachate precisely when Marysville Creek flooded.

***

Fast forward to December 2015. There is disturbing news from the province's renamed Ministry of the Environment and Climate Change. Water samples south of Beechwood Road (south, that is, of the landfill) had shown leachate contamination. Chief Don Maracle had worried that Marysville Creek, which runs south to the Mohawk reserve, could be contaminated, raising fears for wells on the reserve. As it turned out, there were grounds for his concerns.

The Mohawks' consultant engineers had noticed pooling of water on the ground south of the landfill. They observed a sheen on the water surface, suggesting contamination. Based on their observations, they believed that drilling at the site had tapped into an artesian well and caused upwelling of leachate-contaminated groundwater. They noticed the water tracking south to join a rivulet heading west to a culvert that carried the water towards Marysville Creek. The ministry didn't seem concerned and reiterated that its surface water scientist was planning to carry out testing in the spring. To the dump opponents who were farmers in the area, this was not a good idea, as spring flooding might dilute any contaminants that were present.

The leachate plume, meanwhile, inexorably moves south—towards the Bay of Quinte, a picturesque body of water considered a pollution hotspot and designated an area of concern by the Ministry of the Environment and Climate Change.

CHAPTER 11

FRACTURED LIMESTONE

*"Groundwater monitoring in fractured
rock is virtually impossible to carry out reliably."*
—Steve Medd, geologist, 2001

In 1998, Steve Medd went to a public meeting at the Selby Community Hall about a proposal to expand the Richmond Landfill. And with that, a key player in the dump fight entered the scene.

Steve has deep roots in the community but his career, first as a mining exploration geologist and then as an environmental geologist, had taken him all across Canada, Norway, and Germany in the 1980s and early 1990s. In the 1990s, he worked for the Royal Military College in Kingston investigating contamination at the sites of former Canadian military installations. But the travel wore on him, and in 1997 he embarked on a career change—one that would take him out of geology and into information technology. That was more conducive to raising a family. Since 2005, he has worked as the database administrator at Loyalist Collegiate in Belleville. By that time, he and his wife, Kathy Medd, had two young daughters. Whatever sense of stewardship Steve felt for his community's water, land, and air—already deeply felt—was given added impetus when he became a father. What had caught Steve's attention and prompted him to attend the public meeting was the scale of the proposed dump expansion.

In March 1998, Canadian Waste Services, then the dump's owner and a subsidiary of Waste Management Inc., announced its intention to expand the existing Richmond Landfill sixfold, from an annual disposal rate of 125,000 tonnes to 750,000 tonnes—the scale of the proposed expansion was so vast that this number kept going up, over and over again. The dump would also dramatically increase in size—from 40 acres to 237 acres; only after twenty-five years would the proposed mega-dump reach its projected capacity of 18.5 million tonnes.

Provincial government regulations dictated public meetings to discuss the terms of reference that would have to be established. It was one such public consultation meeting that Steve Medd attended. These were also the meetings that so disillusioned Margaret Walsh and Allan Gardiner.

Steve is not a man who would go unnoticed at a rural gathering such as the one at Selby, a village just north of Napanee. There is his size. He stands six feet, two inches tall and weighs more than two hundred pounds. He often sports an Irish cap that matches his salt-and-pepper beard, and he has a fine singing voice. In 1999 and 2000, Steve made two country-folk albums that featured a young Avril Lavigne (once the Medds' babysitter); she would go on to become an international pop star. Lavigne sang lead on both CDs to three spiritual songs that Steve wrote for her, rich in metaphors of nature. The point is that Steve Medd is not fazed by crowds; he is a serious musician and quite comfortable at a microphone.

Steve Medd, geologist and musician, at a dump meeting (November 29, 2005). Photo courtesy of the *Napanee Beaver.*

Finally, he is not a come-from-away, as newcomers to rural areas are sometimes called. Steve and Kathy live in what used to be a storage and blending barn for a tea business that had been built in the nineteenth century by the Daly family. The Dalys had come from Ireland in 1840 and settled near Picton before moving to the Napanee area, where the Daly Tea Company (no longer extant) was born. Steve's grandfather bought the property from the Dalys and converted the barn into a house. After his grandfather died, Steve purchased the house from his estate. Like his songwriting, Steve's passion for the environment is deeply influenced by the future of his children and his United Empire Loyalist ancestors who helped build the town. In rural areas of Canada, it's smart to play the local card. Steve had that one in his pocket.

At the 1998 public meeting, Steve Medd rose to say that he had read the most recent company annual monitoring report, which, he noted, contained little mention of fractures in the rock. Such fractures, Steve told those gathered, could be major conduits for leachate. The company consultant was clearly caught off guard by Steve's comment, for he stood up, turned beet red, and shouted back: "You don't know what you're talking about."

Steve was recalling all this in his backyard on Napanee's Graham Street in the spring of 2015. I was struck by the blue metal roof on his white clapboard house, with a large ornate silver leaf by the front door and vertical sidelights to illuminate the entryway. We proceeded directly to the patio, which afforded a view of sprawling, immaculate gardens. Steve's grandmother had always kept flowers in this space, and Kathy Medd had continued that tradition. I noticed a hand pump. A decoration now, it had served as the only source of water when the Dalys owned the place. It was the third week in May and the mosquitoes more or less left us alone as Steve recalled his early days in the dump fight. As he talked, pink petals drifted softly around us from an old flowering plum tree.

When the company consultant got hot under the collar that night in Selby, Steve had one thought: "What would provoke such a dramatic response? They don't have a clue about fractured systems. And because of the fractures in the rock, liquids in that rock are highly unpredictable. There were implications behind my question."

Fractured limestone. Any Napanee area resident with even a passing knowledge of the Richmond Landfill issue knows what it means. The phrase became part of the local vocabulary—in no small part because it kept recurring in the many, many letters Steve Medd, the geologist, began to write to the *Beaver.* The community was getting an education in dump geology, and he was the professor at the blackboard. Fractured limestone has proved to be the Achilles heel in the complex geology of the landfill site.

Everyone in the community knows that the local dump is a witch's brew. Black plastic garbage bags could contain cans of old lead-based paint after a garage cleanup, the heads of chickens from a culling of the flock, oil- and gasoline-soaked rags, toxic cleansers, spent batteries with nickel, cadmium, and mercury—and all the nasty detritus that remains when modern humans use something and throw it away. The garbage bags eventually break and their contents leak into the soil, to be carried by rain and snowmelt into fractures in the limestone. Then where does the runoff go? Steve Medd, at public meetings and in his letters to the editor, kept hammering the point: be sceptical, be *very* sceptical, of anyone who claims to know with any certainty where that leachate plume is going.

"There are horizontal fractures," Steve told me that day in his garden, "but there are also vertical fractures. Add all the variables and it's a complex system. It's hard to track. I went to that first meeting interested in the geology of the project. I also thought I would help my community. And I got entrenched proving that the dump expansion was a risky venture."

Steve went to great pains the day we met to point out that his activism was not always easy. There were moments of acute stress and depression.

"I started with letters to the editor that were critical of the company," he said. "That hit more nerves. There were caustic rebuttals from senior people at Waste Management, challenging me publicly. I was starting to get uncomfortable. We're talking about the biggest waste management company in the world." Steve never lost sight of the fact that his adversary was a powerful multinational corporation, with one to two billion dollars in revenue at stake. Adding to his discomfort was that Kathy Medd was then running the local Chamber of Commerce, of which the company was a member.

When the press, local and beyond, mentioned Steve Medd, he was typically referred to as "an environmentalist," which, he noted, has "a negative connotation in a small-c conservative town." But Steve was undeterred. "I was just going to speak the truth and use my skill," he said. "And as time went on, I got more politically active." By then, he was no longer referred to as an environmentalist. He had become "an activist."

Steve had stuck his neck out, and he became a target. He admits to losing a lot of sleep over the years. The modus operandi of development proponents in these large, divisive cases is to pick a potential adversary, a key one, and isolate and ridicule them. At the height of the dump fight, Steve got two anonymous calls from people who claimed to be in the waste business trying to dissuade him from further involvement in the battle.

"Were they threatening?" I asked.

Steve paused and chose his next words very carefully.

"Let's just say, they were not friendly," he said.

Still, Steve gave no thought to pulling out. "I know my stuff," he told me. "The truth will win out."

Steve knows his stuff all right. When he was a mining exploration geologist, he managed crews that drilled through thousands of metres of bedrock all across Canada, from the Northwest Territories to Newfoundland. And one thing he knows about bedrock is this: "All bedrock is fractured."

For Steve Medd, the idea of putting a dump overtop fractured bedrock is risky and uninformed; the idea of putting a mega-dump overtop fractured bedrock constituted sacrilege and an assault on the environment.

Here's an excerpt from a letter that Steve wrote to the *Beaver* on January 23, 2002:

> Once again I feel compelled to write . . . in defence of our precious environment. The Salmon River is one of the most pristine rivers that flow into the Bay of Quinte. Its relatively unspoiled beauty, like all of nature's treasures, provides local people with a quiet spiritual solace in a place they call home. . . . The fauna and flora of the Salmon River Valley are rich and diverse. . . . The value of the Salmon River lies not in its use as an open sewer by Canadian Waste Services, but as a world of wonderment and beauty for our children and their children.

November on the Salmon River in Lonsdale.
Photo courtesy of Lutz Forkert.

What had provoked Steve's anger was a draft proposal from the then dump owners to put semi-treated leachate into the Salmon River. Even recalling the moment still got him hot. "How *dare* you?" he put it to me. "This is one of the last unspoiled rivers in our region. My daughters explored that river as children. I realized then that the fight had stepped up a notch. It got me really angry. They were so cavalier."

A measure of the passage of time in the decades-long dump fight is that Steve and Kathy Medd's daughters, Stefanie and Carolyn, are young adults now. The former is in her mid-twenties as I write this and her younger sister is halfway through university. But Steve remembers taking them to concerned citizens' meetings at Reeve Margaret Walsh's office when they were just toddlers, and how they would occupy themselves colouring at Margaret's desk.

"Our approach," says Steve, "was to expose the kids to these issues." One result is that these young women possess an environmental awareness. Another is that when Steve Medd ran for Napanee Town Council in 2014, he ran on an environmental platform. He wasn't successful, but he did garner 44 per cent of the vote against a former deputy mayor with thirty years' experience in local politics. After the municipal election, the *Greater Napanee News* reported that Steve Medd was "more invigorated in defeat than most of the others were in victory."

Just as the dump fight led Steve to run for municipal office, it compelled Ian Munro to run for Napanee Town Council in 2014 and Mike Bossio to run federally in the fall of 2015. The risk is that such candidacies will be dismissed as single issue. Still, engagement in the landfill battle led to civic engagement, and that has to be a good thing.

The other spinoff—and every activist in the dump fight told me this— is that true friendships formed in the battle's wake. "I played a big part in the first battle up to 2006," Steve says, looking back on it all. "But others were doing way more subsequently. What a wide-ranging group. Eric DePoe and Carolyn Butts came on. Janelle Tulloch is our trusty bookkeeper. Mary Lynne Sammon was our librarian. Al Gardiner, Steve Geneja, Margaret Walsh, and Ed File were the elders of the issue. Don Ryan was instrumental in the beginning with his petitions and letters. Chief Maracle of the Mohawks of the Bay of Quinte has been an unwavering ally in the long struggle. And there are so many more dedicated people that I could name. At one point, I hit the wall and I was burned out and depressed. That's when Mike Bossio and Jeff Whan and Ian Munro became even bigger. They pulled me up. I am so proud of this committee. Waste Management has never encountered such a battle."

Maybe it's the singer-songwriter in him, but at one point during the dump fight, Steve Medd, addressing a meeting of Napanee Town Council, offered a metaphor (modified, he later admitted, from David Suzuki's website) to describe the latest development. "I feel," he said, "like we have been on a runaway bus ride where Waste Management has hijacked the bus. We've got the Ministry of the Environment in the navigator's seat without a map, and we're all in the back of the bus trying to grab the wheel. We are at a new boiling point in terms of anger and frustration over this recent twist."

Like many concerned citizens, Steve has paid a hefty price for his involvement in the Richmond Landfill issue—lost sleep; countless hours spent in meetings, protests, and crafting letters to the editor; even wages lost. At one point he took an unpaid three-month sabbatical from work to write a technical report that became a major weapon for local citizens opposed to the mega-dump.

"I have no regrets," Steve told me. "At the end of the day, when I am on my death bed, I won't care about fancy cars or gadgets. The question I will ask myself is, What experiences did I have? Did I stand up for something with my fellow citizens for the greater good and my family's future? What I gained from this were friendships. The people on the committee are my second family. I have huge respect for all these people—they put time and energy into this. We have all also gained an awareness. What happened in Napanee is a microcosm for what is happening around the world. Large corporations get what they need. Major corporations are setting the agenda."

I asked Steve, as I had every activist profiled in this book, what advice he had for a community facing a similar threat. "Open your eyes and hearts," he said. "Don't expect someone else to do the work. Get involved smartly. Find people with expertise and mobilize quickly. Get organized and appeal to people's logic as well as their sense of what's morally right. We are all creatures on this planet and we need to protect our space from generationally long-lasting pollution. We need a vision that goes beyond quarter-term profit. We need to give capitalism an overhaul. It's driven by greed."

We—Steve and Kathy Medd and myself—then all decamped to their living room. "To know me," he said as he went, "you need to know my music." He put on one of his CDs, one called *The Quinte Spirit*; Kathy calls the title song "the anthem for the anti-landfill fight."

It goes, in part:

In my heart there is a place so fair
Where lilacs bloom to sweeten springtime air
On limestone shores of waters I have roamed
The Quinte Spirit now calls me back home
And I've been down Hay Bay before
And up Long Reach along the high shore
Tyendinaga and Deseronto too
I'll be in Napanee someday soon.

CHAPTER 12

THE PLIGHT OF THREE FAMILIES

"The dump stinks. It's as simple as that. . . .
The ramifications on the local land values will be disastrous."
—Kimberlee Shelley, 2002

THE SHELLEYS

Rick Shelley owns a farm of a hundred acres on Callaghan Road, about one kilometre west of the Richmond Landfill. He and Linda got married in 1969 when they were both eighteen and just out of high school. He built their home in 1977, and he and Linda raised three daughters on the new farm, which is adjacent to the family farm where Rick grew up.

Rick says that when his parents were originally looking for a property, they considered one that was for sale at the time, a tract of land that was subsequently bought by Fred Sutcliffe Sr. when he first came to Canada. Instead, the Shelleys purchased the home farm where Rick's brother currently lives, because there was a schoolhouse for their children on the property. Rick speculates that had his parents made a different choice, there might not have been a dump at all.

Rick, who has been living in the area since he was three years old, remembers as a young boy playing around the waters of Marysville Creek, catching frogs and fish. He laments what he calls the "dead state" of the creek today and regrets that his grandchildren are deprived of the pleasure he got from his boyhood activities. He and Linda raised a family on this farm, but their daughters have all left now and are raising their families elsewhere. In 2002, Kimberlee Shelley, Rick's youngest daughter, wrote a letter to Elizabeth Witmer (then Ontario's environment minister) that was published in the April 17 *Beaver:* "The dump stinks," she wrote. "It's as simple as that. If the winds are co-operative on any given day, my neighbours and family can smell the garbage rotting. This is not exactly the sort of area around which one would like to live. The ramifications on the local land values will be disastrous because no one will want to live there."

Back in the 1980s, Rick started a farm with a herd of about twenty Simmental cattle of Swiss origin, known to be suitable for both milk and beef. He raised the cattle for beef and did reasonably well, but from about 1998 to 2008, his cows were plagued with reproductive problems. Calves were born dead, delivered prematurely, or born at term but then failed to thrive. Newborn calves had breathing problems: they were heaving laboriously, panting for air. Some calves were born presumably normal but unable to nurse, and they had to be bottle-fed. Like human babies, they needed to be fed about every two hours, or three if Rick was lucky—and he had to go to work the next morning at Millhaven penitentiary. This situation went on for more than ten years, wrecking him mentally and physically. The events also took a significant toll on his finances. Linda, who had always worked at home, had to take on a job because their financial situation became precarious from the loss of so many calves.

"I suspect that the problems with my calves might be related to the dump, to the air contamination," Rick Shelley told me. "They had great difficulty breathing, especially when the air was heavy with the smell of rotting garbage. Their tongues were hanging out, and they were heaving away." He went on. "I believe my well water has always been fine; my family and my animals drink it. The reason is, I think, because it is a dug well about twenty feet deep in soil with solid clay; the clay filters the water. Of course, when the cows are out on the pasture, they will drink from the streams." He added, "My daughters will not drink the well water here; they drink bottled water."

Rick was disappointed that his neighbours were selling their land to the landfill company and facilitating its expansion plans instead of staying put to fight them. Bert Winter and his father were the first farmers to sell in 1996, followed by others. Between 1996 and 2003, the landfill companies acquired hundreds of acres of land in the vicinity of the Richmond Landfill. Mary Lynne Sammon, who had spent time digging through the land registry office, estimated that it was over seven hundred acres in Concession IV, and about two hundred acres in nearby Concession III.

"They are the ones who are selling the neighbourhood down the tubes," Rick said. "I bought that little farm I got there, my dream place, and I am not going to give that up so that the waste company can make billions of dollars."

THE SUTCLIFFES

Ben Sutcliffe, the nephew of Fred Sutcliffe Sr., has a home and farm just across the road from the landfill. Ben is probably one of the most passionate and vocal opponents of the expansion—in part, because of the financial disaster he has suffered.

He and his wife, Janet, were horse breeders who had immigrated to the area from Britain in 1967. His accent still has a pronounced Lancashire lilt, so that the word *government* coming from him sounds to me like "guviment"; when he talks about Fred Sutcliffe Sr., Ben refers to him as "me favourite uncle." As for farming, Ben says, "It's in me blood." Ben is also a dog breeder. The living room, where we parked ourselves one day early in 2015, is a showcase of decorative porcelain dogs, paintings of proud dogs, and dog show ribbons hung here and there.

Ben and Janet came to the area because Fred was already here—despite the strained relationship between Fred Sutcliffe and Ben's father. Back in England in the 1950s Fred had told his brother—Ben's father—of his intention to apply for a lease on land owned by the Prince of Wales. When this brother immediately applied for the same tract of land, and got it, Fred felt betrayed. That's when he decided to emigrate to Canada.

When Ben Sutcliffe came to this same area looking for farmland, he was told that the dump was closing in three years. Although he was in contact with both his uncle and his cousin, neither told him about the potential dump expansion. At the time, 1986, both Fred Sutcliffe and his son had a copy of the Environmental Assessment Board report—recommending approval of the expansion—but they did not share it with Ben. Not long after Ben bought the fifty-acre farm, one of his neighbours gave him a copy of the report.

He confronted his cousin, Fred Jr., and asked him, "Have you read this report, Fred?" His answer was no. "Why didn't you tell me about the expansion?" Ben asked. "Had I known, I would never have bought this farm." Fred Sutcliffe Jr. did not answer. That was the last time Ben spoke to his cousin.

With delicate phrasing, Ben described how the dump issue damaged their relationship: "I have not fallen out with him but it's impossible to call him a friend. I am ever so slightly disgusted with him." As for his "favourite uncle," Ben does not hold him accountable—as many others do. "I think he thought the original site was safe," Ben told me. "I thought it was safe."

Ben described starting out on the farm: "The house was built and we moved in by 1987. It proved to be everything we had hoped for, because, being a livestock breeder all my life, the only way to be really successful is you have to be able to sell. The farm was very productive and ideally located. Our water was hard, but otherwise okay—for the first nine years."

When he lived in England, Ben held a jockey's certificate from the British Jockey Club to ride National Hunt horses, which he did successfully for many years. He also held a British Trainers and Drivers Permit with the Standardbred and Trotting Horse Association of Great Britain and Ireland. He bred and sold horses throughout the United Kingdom and Europe. I asked why he immigrated to Canada, as he had been highly successful in England. He said, "Yes, we were doing well, but we thought we could do better." And at first that seemed to be the case: horses the Sutcliffes bred in Canada were sold and shipped, mainly to the United States. Their sales kept increasing, and their financial assets mounted. The decision to immigrate to Canada was turning out to be a smart move.

Then in 1996, all their breeding mares either aborted or produced deformed foals. The next three years were productive and uneventful, but in 1999 all the foals once again either aborted or were deformed.

Ben tells a sad story about one of these deformed foals. He was driving by when he noticed that a pregnant mare had separated from the group, indicating that she was about to deliver. Indeed, she had delivered; Ben saw the foal lift up its head above the grass. "I had a moment of elation and thought to myself, 'This is a good one.' On the way back, I stopped and went closer to have a look. The foal was badly deformed. The part below the head looked all twisted, like a corkscrew. It broke my heart. I thought I would have to shoot it, but it died soon after."

When he decided to close down his breeding program, Ben had to get rid of all of his horses. He sold them to another breeder nearby, who contacted Ben to ask him whether he knew that one of his mares was pregnant: the mare had been sold as a "maiden." Ben replied, "No, it couldn't be, because there wasn't a stallion in with the mares at the time." He then remembered there was a young colt of about six months in with his mares. Such a young male would not normally be able to sire a foal; it is usually a year before this is possible.

Ben concluded, "It must have been the young colt. There was not a stallion around." When the foal was born, he went out to have a look, and proclaimed, "This is a beautiful foal. You must use this young colt for breeding." Shaking his head, the breeder said, "Too late! I've already had him gelded." A few days later, the breeder phoned to tell Ben that the foal had died.

Ben discontinued breeding horses in 2000. "It had turned from being a profitable and incredibly pleasurable occupation into a total nightmare," he said. "Our reputation in the horse world had taken a monumental battering, with sales taking a nosedive by over fifty thousand dollars."

He was puzzled and stymied. "I researched all the possible causes I could think of, including the effects that the hydro wires might have across the north end of the property. I could find no reason."

Sometime later, when he read the 1986 Environmental Assessment Board report, he considered the possibility that the dump might be a culprit—that the breeding problems might be related to the water the horses were drinking. Beechwood Ditch runs across the pasture the mares were kept on, and it drains any runoff from the north and east sides of the Richmond dump.

"There is also a spring-fed pond, which is only approximately five hundred metres from the dump," Ben told me. "This pond had always harboured a good population of both fish and frogs, with a blue heron in almost permanent occupation. In the late 1990s, the fish, frogs, and heron all disappeared. The mares also drank from this pond."

Ben continued, "While all this was going on, we were very successfully breeding our Jack Russell terriers. They were drinking the well water at our house, which is at the south end of our farm, approximately a quarter-mile from the dump. In the year 2000, the whole breeding program with the dogs went completely haywire, and we had about a hundred puppies born either dead or deformed. Our well has been so good that it came as a tremendous shock to find out that it was now so badly polluted."

He described the strategy he used. "The well water definitely was the problem, and I started from that time forward to rear the dogs on rainwater, and purchased water for the house." But collecting rainwater was problematic, as their roof was covered in droppings from seagulls on their way to feed on the garbage at the landfill. Eventually the family resorted to giving the Jack Russells bottled water only—an expensive proposition. More recently, he and Janet resumed using rainwater, which no longer presents a problem. "You see, the dump has closed and the garbage is capped. The gulls don't have garbage to pick over for food anymore and are mostly gone. We still have some, though, as there is always garbage around.

"Now," Ben said, "the dogs have returned to almost normal production."

Janet added, "We keep our dogs confined to one area of our property and will not allow them to drink any water from elsewhere or to run free on our land. There are so many dead seagulls and bird droppings on our property, but not as many or as much as there were when the dump was open."

Ben and Janet are proud of their dogs. "Our kennel of Jack Russell terriers is known throughout the world," said Ben. "We sell breeding stock mainly in the United States, but we have also sold terriers to South Africa, Italy, Germany, Netherlands, Singapore, Japan, and many other countries. The ones we sell locally are mainly for pets."

Once Ben and Janet started using bottled water themselves, they began experiencing better health. But since their property is so close to the landfill, the stench of garbage still invades their property and home. They still have breathing problems, with coughing and wheezing and other medical challenges. Janet is plagued with stomach ailments as well as allergies. She was not able to have children, and is ironically thankful. "I would have killed myself if I thought I would have been guilty of producing a deformed child like what we have produced in our deformed horses and dogs," she told me.

Ben returned to the subject of Fred Sutcliffe Sr. "I have never had one single cross word with my uncle; he never found out about the problems he had caused. He was old, and I didn't see any point in raising the issue."

But had Ben known about the expansion, he would never have bought his farm property and thus would perhaps have avoided all the grief that he and Janet have endured. "I do regret buying this place," he told me as I left. "I sold the land to Rob Chadwick, and he uses it just for crops—no livestock. But who will buy the house?"

THE CRANSTONS

Originally from Stirling, Ontario, Douglas and Betty Cranston live on Callaghan Road and own the property next to the Sutcliffe farm. They moved to Napanee in 1962. "This is actually home, this area," said Betty. "We always wanted a farm, and when we got a chance to buy this, we bought it in 1973." They have raised purebred cattle since then. They are upset by what has transpired in their lives and are anxious to tell their story.

Doug worked for the Department of Highways for thirty-five years and retired in 1992 with a full pension. "The idea was to come here and enjoy our life, but needless to say, the last ten years of our retirement have been spent fighting this mega-dump," he said. "When we bought this place, there was a small family-run dump. All that was going in there was what Fred Sutcliffe picked up from Napanee."

Doug and Betty were plagued by the stench of rotting garbage. "We were having the smells all the time, not just outside but also inside," said Doug. "If you were in bed sleeping, you'd have to cover your head."

Betty added, "It was so sour, it would turn your stomach."

Doug described going to the barn one evening to check on the cows, as they were getting close to calving. "I was about halfway there, and I couldn't get my wind. I couldn't breathe, but I finally got into the barn where the stench was not so bad. I checked the cows and finally got back to the house."

Doug said, "Similar to us, our cows have breathing problems with the foul air. When we are bad, they are bad too. When we get better, they get better too. We would be coughing and wheezing, and they would be heaving with their tongues hanging out." The Cranstons noticed that the animals were worse when the weather was hot.

Doug kept a book in which he recorded the dates they were experiencing "smells," and reported them to the Ministry of the Environment; the ministry had encouraged residents to report odour incidents. The family kept on reporting for a year, and the ministry finally said to them, "We're getting too many of these things." Despite all the reporting from the Cranstons and their neighbours, the odours continued unabated. One winter, Doug said, the odours were so bad that he was "raising the devil" with the ministry. He had been complaining for a month and a half when he was told, "Oh, forgot to tell you, those lines were broken and it was leaching out on the top of the ground. We're getting that fixed. It will only be another couple of weeks—we'll have that all fixed up."

For over ten years the Cranstons have had calving problems: deformed fetuses, premature births, and full-term calves that were born dead or died soon after birth. A six-week-old calf became sick soon after birth. The veterinarian came out and treated the animal, and a few weeks later it had to be treated again. He recommended that Doug take it to the animal hospital. When he brought the calf home from the hospital, he put it among the cows. It started nursing normally but in a few days got sick again. So Doug decided to treat the calf himself, administering a cocktail of drugs in his possession. This went on for about two weeks. One day, the calf got out, got caught in the bars of the gate and hung itself. "Another calf was born, nursed once, and died. And another one could not find the feed. I don't really know if she was blind or not, but she wasn't seeing right. She also couldn't find the door."

With typical black humour, Betty added, "Our calves were born dead or stupid."

Doug described another calf: "Half of his head was not as full as the other half, like, if you looked straight on. He lived, we saved him, but it was costing so much I had kind of given up on the vets. I didn't want to spend all this money for nothing. We had quite a lot of medicine on hand, different brands. So we used our own judgment about what we should do and shouldn't do—and we saved him gradually. He got better and he turned out all right."

Betty remembered a strange incident with a woman who claimed to be a reporter from the *Toronto Star*. "This girl came to take pictures. She wanted to see if she could get a picture of the cows in the creek over there. She came for the creek and not for the dump."

Doug wondered if someone was paying this photographer—and he very much doubted it was the *Toronto Star*. "She was just all gung-ho," he said, "to get a picture of the cow going through this ditch with the water in it." Doug speculated that such a photo could be used to show that the cows were tainting the water with manure. In any case, there never was an article or a photograph in a Toronto newspaper.

Doug stayed with the subject of water. "The surface water runoff from the dump that runs across my farm and Ben's," he told me, "produces a mud field. If there's water in the ditches, my cows are going to drink it. One year we had so much it was hard to get the hay off."

He complained to the ministry about leachate in the runoff, and the response was that there was no impact—the leachate was diluted. But when fall came and the Cranstons got the animals into the barnyard, they noticed that the cows' feet were red and raw. They also noticed the same thing with their dog.

"About a month or month and a half that I had the cows in the barnyard, their feet cleared right up. Then I realized what the problem was. It was the water in the ditches. The ditches were not fenced. Nobody fences ditches. The cows were continuously going through the water."

Doug believed there were other impacts in the area. "There were a few birds here in the spring, robins and what have you. But a few weeks into the summer, everything seemed to leave. This ditch over here always had frogs and mud minnows in it, and in the last three years there's been nothing. I think we had about three frogs around the house this year."

Doug had the water in their two wells tested by Canadian Waste Services back in August 1998. He was told that the results showed the water did not pose a health hazard and was safe for drinking. The family continued to use both wells for drinking water. When he later heard that his neighbours were either using a water purification unit or drinking bottled water, he decided that he should do likewise and had a purification system installed. It was then that he arranged to have his water tested by both the company and the Ministry of the Environment. Both called back to say the well water should not be used for drinking due to bacterial contamination. Since his purification system was not an expensive one, Doug decided it was better for his family to use bottled water for drinking and cooking, a practice they continue to this day. For bathing and showering as well as washing, they use water from a cistern that collects rainwater. But their cattle drink the bacteria-contaminated well water. Moreover, the cattle are out on the pasture, drinking water from the streams.

Doug and Betty Cranston became involved with the citizens' group in 1997, when Laidlaw owned the landfill. They kept close watch on the activities at the dump and provided useful information to the group, and lodged complaints to the ministry when they observed effects that would impact the community. The couple kept phoning the ministry, even though they knew little action was taken and not much happened. They felt helpless: "There is nothing we can do. We are just trapped."

Doug Cranston sold all his cattle in the spring of 2013. By then, the Richmond Landfill had closed, but he was still having reproductive problems with his cows. He said, "All the problems with the cattle kind of wears you out."

I met Doug and Betty most recently at a Christmas potluck dinner at Empey Hill church in December 2015. This is an event held every year by the dump opponents. The Cranstons told me that they still have smells from the dump now and then. "They are less often and not as bad as they used to be before the dump closed," said Doug. And Betty added, "I guess we should be grateful for that."

***

In February 2012, an organization called Landfills Anonymous put out a six-and-a-half-minute video on YouTube that chronicles the experience of farm families living in Yamhill County, Oregon, when Waste Management, Inc., converted a small, locally owned landfill into a mega-dump. The experience is eerily similar to what happened in Napanee.

The video, called "Riverbend Landfill: Legacy of Lies," describes how the company promised that local residents would neither see the dump nor smell it. That's not what happened. Farm families interviewed complain bitterly in the film about intolerable smells ("like rotting dead animals," one farmer says), plastic garbage bags and soiled diapers hung up in the trees, plummeting land values, and young riders at a nearby equestrian centre having to wear gas masks. Worse, the company was seeking to expand the landfill right next to the Yamhill River—so pollution of waterways and wells with toxic leachate was an abiding concern.

You can find a link to the video on LeakyLand.com, a website developed free of charge by Heather Scott for the CCCTE. Heather is not directly affected by the area's problems but chose to do the work pro bono "for reasons of social justice." She said, "I refuse to stand idly by while a huge corporation like Waste Management makes enormous amounts of money while potentially placing the health of tens of thousands of Canadians, and our environment, in danger." Jeff Whan now maintains the website.

It's hard to say which dump—Riverbend or Richmond—is bigger. One cheeky entry on the LeakyLand website notes, "The base of this garbage mound covers three times the area of the largest Egyptian pyramids. It holds approximately 3 million tonnes of human refuse and although it holds no mummy, it does carry a curse. The leachate (garbage juice) produced within it is expected to be toxic for approximately 300 years."

CHAPTER 13

THE CHIEF

"There isn't another reserve that we can move to."
—Chief Don Maracle of the Mohawks of the Bay of Quinte, 1999

I'm standing in the light-splashed, cathedral-ceilinged atrium of the new band office of the Mohawks of the Bay of Quinte at Marysville in Tyendinaga Township. It's a stark contrast to the previous band office, which was in a leaky old school building that was frigidly cold in winter. I have a few minutes to wander the entryway as Chief Don Maracle is paged. It's a bright July morning in 2015, and the band office has been open less than a year.

On one wall are almost two dozen black-and-white photographs of Mohawk soldiers who fought for king and queen in the first and second world wars. The photos are not there by chance. The long history of Mohawk military support for the Crown goes back to British redcoat days and the American Revolutionary War, with the grateful royals promising much land in return. Those promises are the subject of negotiations that have dragged on for centuries. The Mohawks have been as determined and savvy in those deliberations as they were in battle centuries ago, which is why every activist in the Richmond Landfill saga concurs: if we have indeed won the fight, we could never have done so without our alliance with the MBQ. The Mohawks of the Bay of Quinte.

I can recall dump meetings when Mohawk warriors came with their flags depicting the silhouette of a warrior in profile with a golden sun behind on a red background. The men first circled the room, and then went to the back to stand, arms crossed, silent, and just a little menacing. The warriors never did or said anything, but they were a presence. A hard-core group of Tyendinaga Mohawks once shut down Highway 401—the busiest highway in Canada—as well as passenger and freight trains for hours back in 2007. The days of protest were meant to bring attention to aboriginal issues such as poverty, suicide, and land claims (hundreds of outstanding land claims are stalled across the country). Don Maracle is more of a suit and tie politician, but he is also a shrewd player, and politicians return his phone calls.

I remember a public meeting at the Selby Community Hall in 2005 when Chief Maracle said that the Mohawks would never allow anyone to "poison the people in their nation." Clearly frustrated, he warned, "So, as part of your risk assessment, you better take into account civil unrest." He paused to let the point sink in. And in a meeting at the Ministry of the Environment in Toronto, I watched him calmly but emphatically say, "Not a single garbage truck will get through. If we have to shut the 401 down, we can do that again." Ministry officials clearly heard the threat. There was a palpable silence in the room.

***

When Chief Don Maracle emerged to greet me, he hugged me warmly, for I have known and worked with him now for more than a decade. We settled into his office at the back of the one-storey, 2,200-square-foot red-brick building with a metal roof the colour of new spring leaves. On the opposite wall was a photograph of the chief meeting the Queen in 2002. Behind the chief as he sits at his desk is a huge window that looks out onto a pastoral scene of trees, wildflowers, and grasses. "Two deer come by just about every morning," he said. "And sometimes foxes."

Immediately, and for the record, Chief Maracle launched into a detailed history of the Mohawks of the Bay of Quinte, who now number almost ten thousand (living on and off the reserve). I already knew some of the history—Chief Maracle thought I should be informed about Mohawk history and had put me in touch with Trish Rae, their historical researcher. The Mohawks were the easternmost members of the Six Nations Iroquois Confederacy. They lived for millennia in Fort Hunter on the banks of the Mohawk River in what is now upstate New York. Their lands became battlegrounds in the American Revolutionary War and their homes and farms were destroyed. They fled to Canada in 1777. He described how they were holed up, under harsh conditions, in Lachine on the St. Lawrence River on territory controlled by their ally, Great Britain. And how they waited seven years for a new homeland the British had promised them.

The chief paused and took a breath, almost a sigh. He glanced at some notes on his desk—he had done some preparation. And then he resumed his narrative.

The Six Nations were granted land in what is now Ontario by treaty—the Simcoe Deed or Treaty 3½.[34] Led by Captain John Deserontyon, twenty families arrived by canoe on May 22, 1784, at the Bay of Quinte, familiar territory, as the area on the north shore of Lake Ontario was their summer hunting grounds. In the decades that followed, white settlement whittled their territory of 93,000 acres, known as the Mohawk Tract, down to 18,000 acres. The first portion of the Mohawk Tract was surrendered in 1820, and by 1850 a vast area of the territory had been lost. The Mohawks have launched land claims to reclaim some of the land they say was stolen from them—they assert that they have never surrendered those lands. Through land claim negotiations they have regained some of the land, which has now been incorporated into the reserve.

As Chief Maracle talked about the four "Mohawk kings" who travelled to visit Queen Anne of England in 1710, I thought of how past and present are so interwoven here. Of those photographs in the entryway, most were of soldiers named Brant or Maracle. Joseph Brant (1743–1807), or Thayendanegea, was a key Mohawk leader and ally of the British; Tyendinaga Township is named after him. He did not settle here, but led a large group of Six Nations to a site on the Grand River.

Don Maracle has been chief of the Bay of Quinte Mohawks since 1993, and he was on council for twelve years before that. Prior to that he worked in Ottawa in finance and administration for Indian Affairs.

Don was born in the Tyendinaga Mohawk Territory, one of twelve children. He and others on the reserve were spared the horrors of the residential school system, but he does remember going to a school in nearby Belleville for grades seven and eight. "I remember first arriving there by bus," he said, "and the other kids encircled the bus and called us 'itchybums' while doing the war whoop with their hands at their mouths. We had friends at the school but some were racist. Some thought we were living in teepees, which we never did. Always they felt superior. We said to them, 'In the 1600s you guys were burning people at the stake and living in castles that were dirty, rat-infested, and cold.'"

The chief never loses sight of two elements. One is what he calls "the three-hundred-year history of Mohawk military allegiance to the Crown." The other is treaties, and the guarantees that were made to the Mohawks about land. I have heard Don Maracle say many times, "They're not making more reserves. We can't go anywhere else. People living in the country north of us, near the dump, can be bought out and move elsewhere. That's impossible for us here." The thought of tainted water slowly and steadily making its way south from the dump towards the Mohawk Territory spurred his predecessor, Chief Earl Hill, into action. And it motivates Don Maracle to continue that action.

Don remembers Margaret Walsh, the former reeve of Tyendinaga Township, approaching him in 1998 about the proposed expansion of the

Richmond dump. Seventeen years later, the cost to the reserve of paying for expert witnesses and lawyers sat at $432,000. But after hard lobbying on the part of the chief, the reserve did get a portion of that amount reimbursed by Waste Management.

When I asked Don to describe some of the high and low points of that seventeen-year-long battle, he sighed. "There isn't one moment," he replied. "Just ongoing anxiety. The whole regulatory process needs an overhaul. The whole system is flawed. The Ministry of the Environment orders the company to do reports but those experts hired to do the reports are, as expected, loyal to their clients. We need independent experts hired by the ministry—not by the company."

If land is a critical issue in the Mohawk Territory, so is water. The chief gave me a grand tour of the reserve, including the new water treatment plant still under construction and expected to be operational in 2016. He had numbers at his fingertips: about 2,150 live in the territory in about 1,060 households. Of these, about 275 have access to municipal water, sewers, and fire hydrants from an extension from Deseronto. The new plant, he told me, will take water from Lake Ontario, purify it, and convey it to homes on the reserve as well as to public buildings. It would be completed in October 2016, and now supplies clean water to some community resources—school, band office, health (wellness) centre, community centre, police building—and forty-eight houses. But 750 homes on the reserve still rely on groundwater wells that can be impacted by surface water, and half that number have been shown to be contaminated with bacteria, including E. coli and parasites. Residents who live in those houses have operated under a continuous boil-water advisory—like on hundreds of reserves across the country. He paused in his narrative about the water situation on his reserve, and added, "We don't need Waste Management to come here to make worse an already bad situation." The new water treatment plant will not provide clean water to all the households currently on well water. I asked Chief Maracle why he didn't lobby for all the households to be on piped water. His answer: "It took nine years for me to get this, and I'm not going to spend another nine years lobbying for the rest. I'll take what I can get now." He stressed that access to clean water for the residents on the reserve is an "incremental process," and it will take many years before all his people will get to live under conditions that are taken for granted outside the reserve.

"The community," Don told me, "will always be at risk. The dump is there. It's a source of pollutants. The water here sits on a shallow aquifer, and there's not a lot of it. It needs protection."

It bothers the Mohawks a great deal that without intervenor funding, band coffers are being emptied to fight against this unwanted development. A host of other issues—a proper secondary school, safe water, housing, health services—also warrant attention. Waste Management has virtually unlimited reserves of cash to throw at the fight and appeared not to be averse, residents believed, to suing either citizens or the government. Margaret Walsh knows all about that threat, and early activists in the dump fight such as Allan Gardiner were fearful that they, too, would be slapped with a lawsuit for speaking out against dump expansion. But it did not deter Allan or others from speaking out or fighting against the company's expansion plans.

"Ordinary citizens should not be subjected to this," the chief said. "The issue is public health and it's grossly unfair to citizens in the area near the dump and here to be put through this process. Waste Management can appeal ad infinitum. As for government, I see the ministry as just a middleman. Why any government would entertain the possibility of a dump on that site . . . it's not rational thinking. It makes no environmental sense. Who comes good for the damage inflicted on private citizens? There's no thought for families."

***

Why were the Mohawks such important allies in the dump battle? I pondered that question as Don Maracle drove me around the reserve that day. One answer is the chief himself. There is a gravitas about the man, a high seriousness that is most apparent when he's on a stage, as he was, for example, during the spring of 2015 when the Environmental Review Tribunal hearings took place and he was on the witness stand. My sense is that he takes his job very seriously and prepares well.

He keeps the other side off balance, sometimes by *not* participating in "public consultation" exercises if he thinks they are a sham—which they sometimes are. The chief, for example, refused to even talk or correspond with the developer during the terms of reference of the environmental assessment process, preferring to speak directly with the Ministry of the Environment.

Sometimes direct action is taken. On September 29, 2000, Maracle, along with the Mohawks of the Bay of Quinte, residents of Tyendinaga Township, and other groups, mounted a massive demonstration. More than two hundred vehicles and hundreds of protesters wound their way from the Tyendinaga Mohawk Territory to the Richmond Landfill. Three members of the provincial legislature—Ernie

Protest caravan of tractors and cars winding its way from the Tyendinaga Mohawk Territory to the Town of Greater Napanee (September 29, 2000). Photo courtesy of the *Napanee Beaver*.

Demonstrators marching from the Tyendinaga Mohawk Territory to the Town of Greater Napanee to protest proposed dump expansion (September 29, 2000). Photo courtesy of the *Napanee Beaver*.

Hardeman, Leona Dombrowsky, and Ernie Parsons—joined the protesters. They handed a three-thousand-name petition against the dump expansion to Michael Walters, Canadian Waste Services division landfill manager, and Jack Varctte, site manager of the Richmond Landfill. Walters accepted the petition from the protesters, and told them that it would be added to the information gathered during the public

Chief Don Maracle leads a massive demonstration of citizens, tractors, and cars from the Tyendinaga Mohawk Territory to the Town of Greater Napanee (September 29, 2000). Photo courtesy of the *Napanee Beaver.*

consultation process. On several occasions, the protesters shouted Walters down, drowning out his words.

The group then proceeded to the Town of Greater Napanee, clogging streets and snarling traffic. Flanked by dozens of protesters, Chief Maracle presented the petition to Mayor Bud Calver and Willliam Weaver, South Fredericksburgh councillor, urging them to abandon support for the proposed landfill expansion. He expressed the opponents' concerns about the expansion, as the protesters carried a mock coffin up the steps of town hall.

Don Maracle's advice to other citizens fighting unwanted development in their communities is not unlike the advice that other activists offered. "Know," he said, "that you are in for a long fight. You better have stamina. You also need experts, and you need funds, lots of it. Know that the company will fight long and hard."

The chief then took me to lunch at a diner on the main street of Deseronto, named for Captain John Deserontyon, the Mohawk chief who died in 1811. The café and indeed much of the downtown and adjacent area are all part of what's called the Culbertson Tract, a 923-acre parcel that has been the subject of land claim negotiations initiated in 2003. But by 2008, negotiations with Stephen Harper's Conservative government had reached an impasse. The government's preferred option was the mandatory surrender of the land and a cash settlement. The Mohawks of the Bay of Quinte insisted on return of the land and compensation for loss of use. The government did not respond to repeated

Dump opponents carry a mock coffin up the steps of Greater Napanee
Town Hall to protest lack of support from town council for their
fight against the proposed landfill expansion (September 29, 2000).
Photo courtesy of the *Napanee Beaver*.

requests for further negotiations. I spoke to Chief Maracle again about
the Culbertson land claim after the October 2015 federal election. He
said that he is looking forward to working with the new Liberal government on Mohawk land claims, and he believes that the negotiations will
be more constructive and likely more productive. And the Mohawks are
reasonably confident they will not have to spend reserve funds going to
court to compel the government to negotiate in good faith, as they did
with the Harper Conservative government. Ultimately, that turned out
to be a frustrating exercise, as the government's response was to ignore
court decisions.

Chief Maracle is hoping that both the land claim fight and the Richmond Landfill fight will be won—in his lifetime. As he looks back on his
life, he said to me, "I have never had a personal life. I have either to go
somewhere or do something. And now I have to work on a platform for the
upcoming election [in December 2015]." But he is dedicated to what he is
doing, and derives satisfaction working to improve the life of his people.
That's what chiefs are supposed to do—take care of their people on the
reserves. And for Chief Don Maracle, fighting Waste Management's landfill expansion plans is an integral part of that duty to protect.

CHAPTER 14

UPS AND DOWNS

"That was the end of Round 1, but there's like fourteen more rounds to go."
—lawyer Richard Lindgren on a landfill-related
Supreme Court decision, 2005

This story went through many twists and turns. But it is possible to boil down the battle to a half-dozen episodes and key dates. In 1986, Environmental Assessment Board hearings consider Fred Sutcliffe's application to expand the dump—and he wins approval. In 1987, Sutcliffe Sanitation Services is sold to Tricil Ltd., the first of several corporate players to arrive on the scene. By 1999, the true measure of the environmental assault on the region has become clear to the ever-more-alarmed activists as expansion plans morph into mega-expansion plans. Citizen activists retain environmental lawyer Rick Lindgren. Now the battle begins in earnest.

The first major point of contention is the terms of reference for the environmental assessment for the proposed mega-dump. What happens to the terms? They were at first approved in 1999 by the Ministry of the Environment before that decision was quashed by the Ontario Divisional Court four years later and finally struck down by the Ontario Court of Appeal in 2004. But that only hints at the turbulence that anti-dump activists faced as the decades rolled by. Defeat followed by victory followed by defeat. And that's just on one front. There were many fronts, and they were often active simultaneously.

There were certificates of approval to be scrutinized. Amendments to environmental legislation to be examined. Audit reports to be read and reread. Peer review teams met, adjourned, and met again. An environmental assessment was developed, submitted, challenged, withdrawn, rejected. Technical reports were issued by the landfill company, and they had to be reviewed and dissected by the citizens—with press releases and interviews to follow. There were trips to Queen's Park, mediation meetings, teleconferences, and all manner of legal jousts—appeals, hearings, decisions made by one court only to be struck down by a higher court. So much paper, so much work. And while the company representatives and those they hired were handsomely paid, the citizens not only toiled without compensation but also had to fundraise and fundraise, sometimes from their own pockets. Their only certainty was that they were on a roller-coaster ride with no end in sight. There were ups, and many downs.

I look back at what was said, for example, after an apparent win—the judicial review in the Ontario Divisional Court in 2003. "This is a significant victory for our community and for all Ontarians," Chief Don Maracle said at the time. "The court decision should ensure that landfill proponents design and undertake comprehensive EA processes that properly consider alternatives to landfilling."

Just one year later, you can sense the devastation in the chief's statement: "We are very disappointed in the Ontario Court of Appeal judgment. Our community's significant concerns about the dump expansion will not be adequately addressed by the narrow environmental assessment process sanctioned by the court." The appeal court was unanimous in its decision to set aside the judgment of the Divisional Court, to dismiss the outcome of the judicial review, and to reinstate the minister's decision to approve the terms of reference. Steve Geneja, one of the early activists in the fight, said he "fell through the floor" when he heard the judges' ruling.

The year 2006 was milestone in the history of the dump fight, and typical of the buffeting that activists took. It was like flying on an airplane through a tropical storm: an exhilarating lift skyward would be followed by a stomach-churning drop. That year, the Ministry of the Environment conducted an extensive review of the expansion proposal at the Richmond Landfill and recommended that the environmental assessment for the expansion not be approved. You can imagine the joy among citizens opposed to the mega-dump.

After many such turns (the Chronology of Events at the end of this book gives a sense of the ebb and flow), the Richmond Landfill site was finally closed in 2011, at which point a new battle presented itself: how to safely close the dump and have proper monitoring plans in place and contingency plans should an unexpected environmental event occur at the site.

Or so it seemed. Fast forward to 2012. A dump expansion plan that was rejected by the province's environment minister, Laurel Broten, in 2006 is still a burning issue, with a very real possibility of a new dump— right beside the rejected one.

On January 19, 2012, the Ministry of the Environment approved Waste Management's application for a public waste drop-off facility at the Richmond Landfill site.[35] The facility was permitted to receive 50 tonnes of waste per day, and to store a maximum of 50 tonnes on any given day. Residents of Napanee, Deseronto, Tyendinaga Township, and the Tyendinaga Mohawk

Territory would be able to deposit household and renovation waste at the site as well as recyclables including electronics, paints, tires, metal, plastics, glass, and cardboard. The waste would not be for disposal at the Richmond site but would be transferred to another landfill for final disposal.[36]

The public drop-off facility was, it appeared, a foot in the door for the Beechwood Road Environmental Centre, as it was called. Of course, landfill opponents were dismayed and angry when the minister of the environment approved terms of reference for an environmental assessment of the centre. Why, they asked, was the ministry entertaining the possibility of a landfill at the site after having rejected the previous proposal? Rick Lindgren was furious.

"The hydrogeology is still the same," he said at the time, "and the surface water regime is still the same. . . . My clients are frustrated and disappointed and puzzled by the minister's approval decision. . . . In my view, this is an ill-conceived proposal at a very environmentally sensitive location."[37]

The testimony of community activists captures their ongoing frustration. Steve Medd watched his daughters grow up as he kept coming out to anti-dump meetings. "Am I going to be bringing my grandkids out to these meetings?" he said. "How long does this have to go on?"

Ian Munro was equally disgusted. "Decisions like this," he said, "make one truly despair for the future of the human species."

***

But whatever despair the landfill opponents felt along the way, their sense of hopelessness never lasted long. Sometimes help came from an unexpected quarter. I think of 2008 when the environmental commissioner of Ontario (ECO), Gord Miller, released his annual report. In it, he commented on the ministry's decision against the landfill opponents' Application for Review.

The latter, filed under *Environmental Bill of Rights* legislation, specifically requests that the existing approvals for the Richmond Landfill be reviewed and amended by the Ministry of the Environment to prohibit any further waste disposal, and any further acceptance of petroleum-contaminated soils after December 31, 2008. The application also requested that Waste Management implement a monitoring and reporting program to determine the nature, extent, and environmental fate of the leachate plume generated at the site. The application was filed with the environmental commissioner of Ontario in October 2008.

In December 2008, the ministry advised the applicants that it was denying the review, as no impacts of off-site groundwater and surface water have been identified. In his report, Miller called the ministry's decision to deny this application "unjustified." He wrote that the ministry's "contention that the 'continued operation of the Richmond Landfill . . . does not have [the] potential for harm to the environment' contradicts the expert hydrogeology opinions provided by its own staff and the applicants."[38]

A group of landfill opponents from the Tyendinaga Mohawk Territory and Greater Napanee—among them Chief Maracle, Mike Bossio, Ian Munro, Jeff Whan, and Steve Medd—were present when Miller delivered his report on October 6, 2009, at Queen's Park. In it he included his concerns about the Richmond Landfill: "Not only is the geology of the area inherently unsuitable for waste disposal," he said, "neither MOE nor Waste Management has identified any pressing need or public good for allowing the site to continue to receive wastes. Since the site currently receives only about 10 per cent of its historical volumes of waste, the ECO does not believe that there would be any undue social or economic hardship to the area if the site were closed."[39]

In an online media conference following the release of the report, Miller added: "The Richmond landfill has been assessed for possible expansion and found to be deficient technically, an improper place to put a landfill site. Now I am trying to bring attention to it. The time has come to close this, and to close this sad chapter in waste management in the province of Ontario."[40]

In an ideal world, that would have been the end of the Richmond Landfill. But as Hercules found with the Hydra, that mythical beast of Greek mythology, cutting off one head meant two would grow back in its place.

As I write this in early 2017, there is great optimism that the landfill beast has indeed finally been slain. On Christmas Eve 2015, the Environmental Review Tribunal handed down its report on the Richmond Landfill and the orders were more than we could have hoped for—more stringent monitoring of the site and minimal contamination of drinking water with leachate. (More on that in chapter 19.) The concerned citizens were jubilant, and yet wary. The committee will go on meeting, will continue to go about its business of issuing press releases and waiting to see what the other side will do. So many times in the past, it looked like the dragon had been slain, and too many times it came back with a vengeance.

CHAPTER 15

THE MAKING OF AN ACTIVIST

"We've won the battle, but not the war, yet."
—Mike Bossio, long-time opponent of dump expansion, 2015

Mike Bossio and his family live in a two-storey, century-old, red-brick house set on nine acres on the edge of Lonsdale, a village some twenty kilometres northwest of Napanee. When I visited in May 2015, the purple and the white lilacs were in bloom and he invited me to take home as many bouquets as I could manage—which I did. Once the hugs had been delivered. Mike is a warm man of Italian heritage with a winning smile, one that rarely left his face even as he chronicled his seventeen-year involvement in the bid to stop the dump from becoming a mega-dump.

"I'm a fighter and an eternal optimist," said Mike. He was wearing a wine-red golf shirt bearing the logo of McGill University (where his daughter Hailey was once a student), and we chatted over coffee under an umbrella poolside in the backyard. The place is quiet, village quiet, but every now and again Mike's lovely rolling laughter erupted.

I had many questions, and he responded with stories—to explain how he came to be living in the village, how he got into politics (the former Tyendinaga Township councillor would run for the federal Liberals in the 2015 fall election), and how he became embroiled in the dump fight. It was while they were both on council that Margaret Walsh and Mike launched a number of public meetings to inform residents about the landfill, and the Concerned Citizens Committee of Tyendinaga and Environs was born out of one of the meetings. I had the sense as he talked of a man learning some hard lessons over time and losing whatever naïveté he had once possessed.

We talked about a trip some of us made to Toronto in 2005 to look at Ministry of the Environment documents on the landfill expansion. With us were other citizen activists—Jeff Whan, Ian Munro, and Marilyn Kendall. Mike recalled that we simply contacted the ministry and stated that we wanted to review the public file on the Richmond Landfill expansion environmental assessment. These files are on the public record, and anyone is entitled to access them at any time. Ministry officials provided the documents readily. More recently, the ministry is less welcoming to civic participation; it now requires a Freedom of Information application and identification of specific documents before providing access. This process can result in delays, sometimes past deadlines when the data and information are needed.

We were all curious about the content of the residents' letters to the ministry, as well as reviews of the technical experts from the ministry and other government agencies. The letters, especially from people living near the landfill, were heart-rending. Describing the impacts of the landfill on their day-to-day quality of life, residents pleaded with the ministry not to approve the expansion. I asked a ministry official involved with the file how he felt when he read these highly emotional letters. He said he focused on the legislation. That's one way to deal with it, I concluded.

"We thought," Mike said, looking back on this time, "that if we just got the Ministry of the Environment involved, they would be the cavalry to our rescue." That quaint notion did not last.

"I remember," Mike said, "meeting in a church basement in Napanee with Ministry of the Environment officials. We were devastated. They were hostile witnesses. They thought it completely acceptable that a dump liner would protect the environment, that it was technically feasible. The ministry was claiming that a liner would last for 350 years and Waste Management was saying it would last a thousand years. And there was that fire at the Richmond Landfill in 1998. Allan Gardiner, who called the Fire Department, raised serious concerns about the integrity of the liner. I researched liners. The Environmental Protection Agency in the U.S. looked at fifty landfills thought to be safe. Each one was leaking."

Mike Bossio would come to chair the CCCTE, so he was often the one quoted in the press and he had to stay up to speed. He had been to countless public meetings, participated in many protests, and read countless legal and technical documents. Such involvement gave him an intimate understanding of the dump approval process, and he's convinced the system is tilted.

"The company controls the process," Mike told me. "We are so development driven that corporate interests take precedence. If it wasn't for the Environmental Review Tribunal [which was close to winding up as we chatted], we still would not know what is going on at that dumpsite."

Premier Mike Harris gutted the *Environmental Assessment Act*,[41] said Mike Bossio, adding that Stephen Harper did the same thing at the federal level. Ontario's Liberal government, he noted, has done nothing to address the problem. In 2004, the Dalton McGuinty government established a Minister's Advisory Panel to provide recommendations on improving Ontario's Environmental Assessment Program.[42] The recommendations

Mike Bossio and son Lucius protesting the proposed
landfill expansion on a cold winter's night (February 16, 2000).
Photo courtesy of the *Napanee Beaver.*

in the report, which was made available to the public in 2005, were never implemented. Worse, the Ministry of the Environment has seen its staff sharply reduced over the years, so the expertise to expose risky environmental ventures is stretched perilously thin.

As Mike recalled the shock of some of the low points in the battle ("there were many"), it was as if he was reliving each moment. The sting still seemed fresh.

"It was unprecedented," he said. "The company lost an expansion proposal in 2006 on the basis that the expansion posed a risk to public health and safety, and had a high potential to contaminate the local drinking water. It took more than four years before the ministry forced closure of the old dump in 2011. And for the first time in Ontario history, a company had lost an environmental assessment and came right back to ask for another one with virtually the same proposal as the first one. And yet they did. Right next to the one that had just been rejected. And unbelievably, the Ministry of Environment has approved the terms of reference for the second proposal."

***

Mike Bossio grew up in Toronto but in 1967, when he was seven, his father bought a hotel in Madoc, north of Belleville. In some ways, the move was a disaster. The family barely eked out a living, and young Mike, the odd kid out in a mostly WASP town, was bullied. On the other hand, he loved growing up in the countryside and has fond memories of star gazing in the small hours and hiking in the woods. The experience stamped him in two ways: he would develop a strong sense of what constituted injustice, and he would develop a deep feeling for small communities and the surrounding environment.

As a young man, Mike was an odd-job Jack. He stacked shelves in a grocery store, washed dishes in a restaurant, was a shoe salesman and even a disc jockey for a while. Then one day he spotted an ad for a recruiter, and he began working as a head hunter for technical staff to work in the food, pharmaceutical, and high-tech industries. The money was good, and a less ambitious man would have stayed put.

Not Mike. He decided to continue with his work while pursuing a philosophy degree at York University. "There was a phone booth at the university," he recalled, laughing at his own story. "In between classes, I would get in there with a pocketful of quarters and resumés at hand. I made placements my first week as a recruiter and earned seven thousand dollars. Then nothing for three months. By the end of the school year, I was getting four hours' sleep. How did I do it?" It's a measure of his drive and determination that he did.

Then Mike got into selling telecommunications equipment. The degree in philosophy actually came in handy here. "Philosophy taught me conceptual thinking," he said. "I would go home and design a network."

He was good at the job and almost moved to the United States, but decided instead to go back into recruiting. By then, he had a wife, Irene, and two children, Lucius and Hailey. They were living in Toronto in 1994 and were looking to move. A house in Kingston seemed just the ticket but, as Mike put it, "We thought, let's see what our money will get us in the country. A friend of Irene's had spotted a house for sale in the village of Lonsdale. The first time I set my eyes on Lonsdale, I thought, 'Oh my, this is Brigadoon, I have to live here.' The minute we stepped inside, we said, 'This is the house.' We put in an offer that day."

Now serendipity comes into play. The house had previously belonged to John Walsh, son of Margaret Walsh—then a council member for Tyendinaga Township and an early stalwart in the dump fight. When Mike bought it in 1994—he moved in on an uncharacteristically warm day in December, as he remembers wearing a T-shirt—he knew nothing of wells and septic systems. That meant he was on the phone a lot to John, and that, in turn, brought him into contact with Margaret. They became good friends.

"You should run for council," Margaret urged Mike in 1997. And he did. He was on township council from 1998 to 2001.

In those days, a Mike Harris notion called market value assessment was in vogue, and it mightily irked Mike Bossio. "It got under my skin," he said. "They were passing along tax advantages to large corporations at the expense of residents. I lived in a hundred-year-old house. By Harris's logic, I should pay *no* taxes!" So he got a petition going. And while there was some opposition (Mike Bossio had lived in the community all of three years), some keen local allies sided with him—including Margaret Walsh and master ceramicist Harlan House.

When Waste Management came to make their proposal on the Richmond Landfill expansion, Margaret Walsh, now reeve, and Mike Bossio looked at company representative Kevin Bechard and said, "You want to do *what* on fractured limestone?" That's how Mike describes his reaction on first hearing about the proposed expansion. "We played along with the company and I said, 'Educate me.' Then I went back to Margaret and I said, 'This is a nightmare we cannot let happen.'"

Mike was by then a veteran headhunter running his own successful home-based business; he was used to dealing with big corporations and high-powered executives. He was comfortable speaking his mind in front of a large crowd, and he was smart, tech-savvy, and not easily intimidated. He was, in other words, a very useful ally to all those opposed to a ruinous plan for a monster landfill.

At one point, Mike took the dimensions of the proposed mega-dump and overlaid them on a map of Napanee: "It covered most of the town," he said. "This was the size of the footprint." What a brilliant way to drive home to locals the impact of the proposed landfill.

I asked Mike to imagine that he was a schoolteacher and to grade the major players in the dump fight. He gave Waste Management an F. "They have done all in their power *not* to find leachate," he said. Mike remembered going to the dumpsite with Kevin Shipley, an engineering consultant hired by the Mohawks of the Bay of Quinte. His water samples from a north pond on the site showed evidence of leachate; Waste Management's data, on the other hand, were clean.

That was odd, Mike said. "They used mayonnaise jars to collect samples. I was there. I saw the labels on the jars."

To explain the findings of leachate, the company alternately blamed opposition mistakes in collecting samples or a small abattoir—closed in 1998—that had existed nearby. The latter was clearly a hollow claim, Mike insisted, since abattoirs don't use solvents—the chemicals would have contaminated the meat. So the company's claim that "there's not a lick of leachate going anywhere" met stiff resistance from Mike Bossio and others who were growing increasingly sceptical about assurances coming from both the developer and the government.

"Anyone in this area knew about fractured limestone," Mike said. "Drill ten feet one way and ten the other way and you can get a different result. It's like finding a needle in a haystack. How do you know which fracture has the leachate? Where are the pathways? We don't know." Mike remains angry that Waste Management was so slow to admit the existence of a leachate plume and so slow to warn families living near the dump that their water supply was contaminated.

Mike Bossio refrained from giving the province's Ministry of the Environment a failing grade because they did, in the end, deny the landfill expansion. He also had praise for the ministry's hydrogeologist, Kyle Stephenson: "He has acted for the public interest."

Mike looked back on the battle and the toll taken. "I've been here twenty-one years," he said. "Had someone told me I'd be fighting a dump for seventeen years, I'd say, 'You're crazy.' From the beginning, people told us we were wasting our time, that we were never going to defeat the world's largest waste company. The chips are stacked against us because corporate interests take precedence. And the Ministry of the Environment sees its job as negotiating what's acceptable—not protecting the environment. But we have proven the naysayers wrong; it's tough but you can win the good fight. As one member of our team, Jeff Whan, said on many occasions, 'We are on the side of the angels.' We've won the battle but not the war, yet."

I took Mike to say that those in the community who have fought so hard for so long with so little should feel good about pushing back against a waste giant with virtually unlimited resources. On the other hand, the cost has been high on the community side. "Fatigue has set in," Mike said. "A core group of individuals and interests has uncovered just how wrong that dumpsite is, but you need new people and reinforcements as the thing evolves over the years. It's unjust and unfair that a tiny community has to fight the world's largest waste company—and, to a certain extent, the government. The struggle consumes people's lives, it consumes community resources, so the toll is physical and emotional and psychological and financial. For no other reason than greed."

Mike also looks at the issue from a broader perspective. "Our political system," he argued, "has been hijacked by urban interests at the expense of rural interests." The true cost of consumption, he said, is not being considered.

In the meantime, he offered this advice for anyone battling unwanted development. Either sacrifice your community or fight the tough fight. Organize. Promote the *no* side. Fundraise, fundraise, and fundraise some more! Find experts. He might have added, *befriend* the experts. Hydrogeologist Wilf Ruland has served as an expert witness for anti-dump activists for many years, but his home is in Dundas in southwestern Ontario. One evening in 2010, he was about to leave a meeting in Lonsdale at 11 p.m., intending to drive all the way home—almost three hours away.

"Wilf," Mike told him, "stay at my house. You can drive home in the morning." And the two men have maintained that custom since. Just as Mike Bossio and Wilf Ruland and I and others on the community side have retreated to local watering holes either to commiserate or to celebrate after defeats and victories in this interminable battle.

"That's the best thing about the dump fight," Mike said. "The friendships formed."

CHAPTER 16

GRASS ROOTS

"Enough is enough, Mr. Bechard. The intelligence of the people in this community has had enough insults.... You and Canadian Waste Services don't give a damn about the Salmon River and the environment."
—Ed File, retired York University professor, to a Waste Management official, 2002

It's hard to determine the impact of a letter—to the editor of a local news-paper, to a local politician, to the captains of local industry. Not long after being enlisted in the campaign to stop the Richmond Landfill expansion plan, Rick Lindgren urged concerned citizens to get involved, and they did. They bombarded local newspapers with letters about the impacts of the existing landfill and condemned the proposed expansion. The *Napanee Beaver* published them; so did the the *Napanee Guide* and, to a lesser extent, the *Kingston Whig-Standard*.

In a letter to the *Beaver* on April 14, 1999, Bernice Thompson, a resident of Selby who had frequently attended meetings on the dump issue, wrote:

I have lived in Tyendinaga Township my entire life—my parents and my grandparents before me. My grandparents bought the property in 1900, nearly 100 years ago. This property is less than a kilometre from the Richmond Landfill in Greater Napanee. My father spoke of building Empey Hill Church in 1912. . . . During the depression, because we had no car, we walk[ed] to Empey Hill and became members. This beautiful country church has been the centre of this community for many years. It was built on a hill. Now this hill seems only like a little knoll with the huge moun-tain of garbage at the Canada Waste Landfill site. The scenery and tranquillity have been spoiled. This part of the countryside will deteriorate. The property that my forefathers and their neigh-bours worked so hard for will be of no commercial value.

Bruce McBain of Marysville, on March 27 of the same year, addressed this letter to the *Beaver*: "The Ministry of the Environment would like to suck and blow at the same time. The Ministry will punish farmers who allow their livestock . . . to drink in rivers. At the same time, the same Ministry allows a poisonous leachate plume of liquid-like ooze to pool and fester beneath the Richmond dump." McBain and his family had left the Burlington area and moved to Lonsdale, a picturesque hamlet north of Napanee on the Salmon River. After restoring a former general store as a bookstore, Watermark Books, he watched the business grow and settled down to enjoy the peaceful country life. Before he could celebrate the first anniversary of his relocation, he received a notice announcing the landfill expansion, and he soon learned that the original dumpsite was unlined.

In a letter to the *Napanee Guide* on September 10, 1999, McBain said, "Not only is the leachate plume leaking under Cell 1 [Sutcliffe's original dump site], it's under the entire dump. It's under all existing cells to a depth of maybe 30 inches. This is highly toxic water which I call liquid ooze, and it's loaded with heavy metals." The days of allowing his children to swim in the Salmon River were over. "Now I don't want them near the river," he wrote. "The Salmon River is only seven kilometres from the landfill, and given that the garbage was dumped and stored on fractured limestone, it could not be predicted where the leachate could travel. It could possibily reach the river." (The leachate could be in the river, or not. The testing to date has not been done. In the meantime, McBain does what both industry and the regulating agency should have done: he errs on the side of caution.)

The other side, of course, begged to differ. Kevin Bechard (then with Canadian Waste Services) moved to reassure area residents. In comments to the *Beaver* on April 14, 1999, he maintained that the old section of the dump was working exactly as designed and that no leachate was leaving the site. "Leachate from the Richmond landfill's oldest section has not, and will not," he said, "have any off-site impacts on water quality."

Residents remained unconvinced. Tyendinaga Township resident Paul Finkle told the *Beaver* that an ad campaign conducted in the newspaper saw some six hundred letters sent to the Ministry of the Environment. But Finkle lamented that Greater Napanee council members "won't listen to us. They are staying quiet." Councillors had not supported the anti-dump citizens, and to that point had maintained a distinctly neutral stance.

Dump opponents began posting signs with such slogans as "Stop the Dump" and "Napanee Dump City" around the town and countryside. Some of these signs were visible from Highway 401. That got council's attention. Greater Napanee deputy reeve Gord Schermerhorn said he was outraged to see one when he arrived home from a trip. "The town didn't deserve the title of 'Dump City,'" he said. "We've tried over the last two years to promote this town."

Dump opponents responded to the lack of support from town council by picketing the mayor's levee early in January 2000. According to Steve Kennelly, a vocal opponent of dump expansion, the group concocted the idea on the morning of the levee. After a few phone calls, the protest took shape. While about a hundred supporters of council gathered inside the hall, fifty or so protesters stood outside in minus-forty-degree temperatures carrying signs and chanting "Stop the dump." A few added, "Dump the mayor."

All of this prompted an editorial in the *Napanee Beaver*:

> So, Greater Napanee Mayor Bud Calver thinks that the prevalence of dump signs cropping up in his community are "disgusting." Certainly we agree with Mayor Calver and his councillors that these signs do reflect poorly on the town's image. By posting signs and holding protest rallies, these citizens are raising awareness—the first step in getting people onside for the coming environmental hearing fight. Rather than criticize people for getting involved, council should be standing up and applauding these citizens for taking an interest in the community they call home.[43]

Demonstrators in front of Greater Napanee Town Hall on a cold snowy night (February 16, 2000). Photo courtesy of the *Napanee Beaver*.

***

Those opposed to the dump, it seemed, could not rely on the support of local politicians. The support was there, then it wasn't. Residents were livid when it was disclosed in 2005 that the mayor, three councillors, and the town's chief administrative officer had taken an all-expenses-paid three-day trip, hosted by Waste Management. Three other councillors had declined the invitation. The travellers had toured the company's waste disposal facilities in Quebec and New Hampshire, two among the 250 landfill sites then operated by the company.

Councillors claimed that they had not been influenced, but town residents were sceptical. Don Ryan was stunned. "I can't believe it," he said. "It's incomprehensible that they would simply let Waste Management pay for a trip to Quebec or Vermont or wherever they went and not report it to anybody." Council, he said, had lost all credibility. "I feel that they're in direct conflict. Who are they representing—the citizens of the town or Waste Management?"[44]

Obviously, the mayor and councillors should have predicted that disclosure of their actions was inevitable, and they should have foreseen how people would react. Paul Schliesmann, an editorial writer for the *Whig-Standard*, called the incident "A case of bad judgment." He suggested two courses of action to correct it. "When the time comes to make any decisions about the Richmond Dump, the councillors who went on the trip must either declare a conflict of interest and abstain from voting or pay back the cost of their trip—out of their own pockets—before they vote."[45] Many citizens in the town agreed.

Meanwhile, volunteers for the Citizens Against the Richmond Expansion group had been collecting signatures for a petition to be sent to the minister of the environment. In a letter published in the *Beaver*, Don Ryan, chair of CARE, described the project's scale. "The campaign started with the printing of thousands of petition forms and the monumental task of getting them signed, collected and entered into a database. We collected signatures on the streets, at churches and from door to door canvassing. We had organizers working in the Mohawk Territory, and collected signed petitions from Picton, Arden, Odessa, Belleville and Kingston and surrounding areas."[46] In one area of Napanee canvassed door to door, he said, 98 per cent of those asked signed the anti-dump petition.

On the Monday night council meeting of June 27, 2005, Howard O'Connor presented the findings of the CARE group's petition campaign, saying, "I wish to inform you that approximately 85–95 per cent of the residents of Napanee are opposed to the expansion." He told council that the information could be used in the future for a referendum.

"There were over 3,500 petitions presented to the Minister of Environment, Leona Dombrowsky," he said. "Our extensive survey confidently confirms that the vast majority of residents in Napanee are categorically opposed to the Richmond dump expansion."[47]

***

In contrast to the negative responses of municipal officials to dump opponents, provincial politicians supported dump opponents' efforts—at least in the early days of the fight. Gary Fox, provincial representative for Prince Edward–Lennox–South Hastings, said he did not welcome the landfill expansion. "Personally, I don't think it's such a great idea," he told the *Beaver* in 2000. "I think there are better alternatives than to make a mountain of garbage at that site."[48]

At the same time, Prince Edward–Hastings representative Ernie Parsons unveiled a campaign, complete with postcards and posters, at a press conference at his Belleville constituency office. "[Premier] Mike Harris needs to understand that my constituents are not willing to support any expansion that will potentially jeopardize the quality of their water and the value of their land," said Parsons. He said he had received no response from provincial environment minister Tony Clement after handing him two petitions to stop the dump expansion, both of which had fifteen thousand signatures.[49]

***

The volume of the letters, their bitterness, their sense of loss and betrayal, their cumulative weight—all had their impact. A citizen living in the environs of Napanee did not have to read every environmental audit or environmental assessment or technical report to follow the dump expansion issue. All they had to do was scan the letters section of the local papers.

In 2006, CARE published a 114-page ring-bound book called *Our Community Speaks* that gathered some of those letters, along with newspaper articles and op-ed pieces. In the preface, Marilyn Kendall expressed her hope that "this compilation will not only summarize the numerous areas of concern but also portray the strength and tenacity of the opinions expressed." She described the document as an attempt to rectify the refusal of decision makers to hear the voices of the opposition—"to provide the human face that has been subsumed by convoluted and contestable technical arguments and big-business spin."

Our Community Speaks makes for a fascinating read. A five-page letter signed by eleven local doctors quotes the U.S. Environmental Protection Agency to make the point that all dumps emit leachate into the water, soil, and air—and that one dump in Europe continues to ooze leachate even though its last known users lived during the time of the Roman emperors.

The board of directors of the Kingston and Area Real Estate Association wrote to a Napanee realtor to say that the proposed dump expansion would both harm the local environment and negatively impact property values. A copy of that letter is in *Our Community Speaks.*

In 2005, as the book chronicles, CARE ran ads in the *Napanee Beaver* urging citizens to "Let Laurel Know"—referring to Laurel Broten, then the province's minister of the environment. Send a letter, sign a petition, email the minister, the ad urged, while noting that Tuesdays were "Fax Day" and Thursdays were "Email Day." CARE officials, all volunteers, promised to forward to the minister's office every fax and email sent to them.

A ministry official later estimated that his office had received more than eight thousand submissions—the most ever received by the ministry. Among them was a letter written by CARE's chair, Don Ryan, who described his grandson boarding a day camp school bus one July day and almost retching because the stench of rotting garbage was so bad— this at venues some five and six kilometres east of the landfill. "The whole town was engulfed," Ryan wrote, adding that this was no seasonal matter. A girl living near the dump was physically ill as she got off a school bus the previous Christmas—again, due to strong odours from the dump.

The photographs in *Our Community Speaks* capture the many protests sparked by the dump expansion proposal, including one showing protesters at a public meeting looming over the backs of seated Ministry of the Environment officials while holding a 1.5-metre-wide sign that read: "Waste Management: You Are Not Welcome!"

Handwritten letters from children collected in the book include one from Shayla Moore, who wrote Minister Broten: "Our dump is so high it's like a ski hill."

Finally, near the end of *Our Community Speaks* is an ad inviting readers to come to CARE's Napanee office to examine a Greenpeace book called *Waste Management, Inc.: An Encyclopedia of Environmental Crimes & Misdeeds.*[50] The title says it all.

***

Ian Munro clicked his fingernails on his coffee mug while his wife, Marilyn Kendall, dipped in and out of the conversation to retrieve old clippings or binders of material on the Richmond Landfill fight. It was the first of June, 2015, and we were sitting at their dining room table with its splendid view of the Napanee River and admiring a crimson-red cardinal flitting in the branches on the riverbank.

Citizens protest at a meeting in which officials from the Ministry
of the Environment (seated) are present (November 25, 2005).
Photo courtesy of the *Napanee Beaver*.

"Our dump is so high it's like a ski hill," writes schoolgirl
Shayla Moore in a letter to Laurel Broten, minister of the environment.
Photo courtesy of Lutz Forkert.

The couple was remembering all the dump fight meetings that were held here, with men and women sitting around this same table. They described how activists formed groups, how some of the early leaders were "firebrands" who disagreed over strategy, how splinter groups formed, and how for many months during a seventeen-year span, the fight consumed them both.

"It was a full-time job," said Ian. "Twelve- and fourteen-hour days."

"In a strange way," Marilyn said, "I miss those days."

Like veterans who lament all the terrible aspects of war, this couple was also conceding that there is no denying how terribly alive pitched battles can make you feel.

Marilyn has worked as a writer and editor. She first became involved in the dump fight in 2003. By 2005, she was writing a weekly column, "Discourse on the Dump," for the *Napanee Beaver,* which educated the public on all aspects of the issue. She also helped write and edit numerous related documents such as letters to the editor of local newspapers, the minister of the environment, and ministry staff, as well as numerous flyers and handouts. She remained a member of the communications committee that she helped form in 2006. When the group became somewhat established, they voted in Jeff Whan as chair. Her task was often to boil down a long list of responses to something Waste Management had posted into a five-hundred-word press release. No mean feat.

Ian Munro, for his part, was pulled in after reading company documents and being appalled by their patronizing tone—and immense amount of padding. "I don't consider myself an activist," he told me that day (though he did admit to being a tree hugger). "But I'm a logical thinker and this lies at the heart of why I became involved. The company documents were pathetic. They were *so* bad. I have a master's degree in engineering. I understand three-syllable words."

Marilyn was especially irked by what she called "the boilerplate stuff" in the company documents. Waste Management seems to hire many of the same people as consultants and they tend to offer the same one-size-fits-all assurances.

"The core attitude," said Ian, "is this: *We are Waste Management. Trust us. You are Hicksville, Ontario.* And they still have that attitude."

Ian and Marilyn have lived for the past nineteen years on their three-quarters-of-an acre property on the river—they moved to Napanee in 1997. Ian was forty-two at this point; for twenty-two years he had been an air force engineering officer in the Canadian Forces (his specialty was ammunition and ammunition safety), work that took him across the country and even saw him posted for a while in Australia. He got what he calls "the copper handshake" from the military in 1995 when he was forty. These days—when he's not on dump duty—he is a consultant to the Canadian Department of National Defence, NATO, and the United Nations. He also maintains and restores vintage cars, and goes to car races with Jeff Whan, another car enthusiast.

The couple own a small houseboat named *Hubris*. During a hiatus in the Environmental Review Tribunal hearing, Ian took the boat out to traverse the length of the Trent Canal. Marilyn stayed home but went out to Peterborough the day before the last session. She drove him back to Napanee so he could attend the last day of the hearing (June 22, 2015)—he never missed a day and was an assiduous note-taker.

As I listened to Ian and Marilyn, it struck me that a pitched environmental battle such as the Richmond Landfill is a process that unfolds over time. This couple were changed by their involvement. Whatever naïveté they possessed about the workings of government and industry was driven out of them. *So*, I heard them say, *this is how the world really works*.

Ian, for example, described how early on he maintained a discreet distance from the landfill issue. He read Waste Management's ads in the *Beaver*. "It all seemed fine," he said. But then Marilyn convinced him to attend a meeting in 2003 when the environmental assessment for the proposed expansion was the issue of the day. More meetings followed, and Ian became increasingly unsettled as it sank in: there was a profound disconnect between what the company was saying and what its detractors were saying—and the latter bunch were making far more sense.

For Ian, the problem goes right back to the moment when a waste services giant (Tricil) bought the dump property from Fred Sutcliffe in 1987. Why, Ian wanted to know, did the provincial Ministry of the Environment approve the massive expansion of the dumpsite? This, despite a flawed process that same ministry had presided over. And why did Waste Management, when it came along, not do due diligence before buying the landfill when it was so precariously perched on famously fractured limestone? He calls the purchase "a pig in a poke," and he suspects that the company may have regretted the move. This seemed unlikely, though, as the company kept on buying more and more land. It certainly underestimated the community's will to fight back.

"The Richmond Landfill is an abomination," Ian told me. "There was something really strange about how that approval to expand the site was granted. Fred Sutcliffe is a farmer with a private dumpsite, he applies to the government for an expansion—gets it, and immediately sells the dump and land. And we end up with a mega-dump: with big chunks of it unlined and the parts that are lined are dubious. And where is the Ministry of the Environment in all this? The ministry's own water experts raised concerns about potential water quality impacts with an expansion back in the late 1980s, yet they approved it anyway. In the history of Ontario, only two environmental assessments have been rejected; and ours in 2006 was one. It's true: the dominoes needed to fall just so."

Both Ian and Marilyn count among their closest friends the folks who opposed the landfill expansion, people such as Steve Medd, Mike Bossio, and Jeff Whan. "A huge benefit," says Ian, "is that we made many great friends through this process."

But the point that Ian and Marilyn both returned to again and again as we chatted that day was their rude awakening. Marilyn recalled a visit to the Ministry of the Environment offices in Toronto and losing any confidence she had previously had that the ministry was making sure that environmental assessments were closely monitored and that the environment was protected.

Ian likewise had assumptions dashed. "I flipped completely," he said. "I used to believe the Waste Management gloss. And I was sure that government was there to make sure this was okay. Then I read the documents. We were told that leachate was not moving from the dump. Now it's a kilometre away. I am convinced that had the citizens of this community not stood up, we would have 750,000 tonnes of garbage coming from Toronto. We'd have a twenty-year landfill, a legacy landfill."

The Beechwood Road Environmental Centre, the company's name for the latest iteration of a landfill, is, as Ian puts it, "such garbage." The focus is meant to be on recycling, but if you read the document, as Ian has, you see that the plan is for fifty thousand tonnes of recyclables—and four hundred thousand tonnes of garbage. He calls BREC "a pig with lipstick on it." Other "lipstick" features include processes such as recycling, composting, and conversion of landfill gas to energy.

***

It's clear that vast chunks of time were spent by Ian and Marilyn on this issue. Of all those who fought the dump expansion, they are the only ones who came on board as a couple. In other cases, someone stayed home—to cook the meals, run the errands, and do the laundry. But for Ian and Marilyn, this was a total household commitment that continued for twelve long years and continues to this day. Ian's job was to assess and critique the documents being issued by the company or the government or by various boards and tribunals. He chairs the CCCTE's technical sub-committee, which has the mandate to identify, locate, obtain, read, digest, and report on all landfill-related technical and regulatory documentation. Marilyn's job was to help craft a response that was plain spoken and comprehensible to decision makers and to people in the community—people who were not living the issue as Ian Munro and Marilyn Kendall were.

Like all successful citizens' groups, they got organized. Each member of the communications committee was assigned a target audience. Jeff Whan, for example, was to communicate with the Ministry of the Environment. Ian Munro was to establish a link with the mayor of Napanee and the director of the ministry's Environmental Assessment and Approvals Branch.

Marilyn remembered travelling to the ministry offices in Toronto. "We made them bring out stacks, huge environmental assessment files and thousands of letters. We were in their faces all the time."

Ian was there, too, and he wanted a meeting with James O'Mara, then director of the Environmental Assessment and Approvals Branch of the Ministry of the Environment. Impossible, Ian was told. But he got his meeting.

There's a lesson here for other citizens suddenly cast into the role of activists. "One thing we did," Ian noted, "is that we refused to allow decision makers at the Ministry of the Environment to be anonymous. We dragged them to meetings to explain the process. We made them justify their actions and decisions. It put the landfill issue higher up in their consciousness as they sat in their little cubicles."

Ian's counsel to citizens is to throw everything at your opponents, kitchen sink included. "My advice to a group facing a situation similar to ours is to do all you can think of," he said. "It's death by a thousand cuts. Letters, petitions, public meetings, phone calls, protests. Ours was such a collective effort. I remember Christine Silver, a woman in her sixties. She collected all the newspaper clippings for us and jealously guarded the books she stored them in. Hundreds of people did work behind the scenes—baking, making coffee, organizing dances, selling raffle tickets, collecting signatures. And the never-ending fundraising projects."

The formula for success here is pretty simple. "Get smart people," Ian said, "and keep working."

Marilyn observed that it's important not to feel overwhelmed and overawed by big companies with big money. I suggested that Chief Don Maracle of the Mohawks of the Bay of Quinte showed no fear and, indeed, showed the way.

"The MBQ contribution," Ian agreed, "cannot be overstated. The chief was part of the citizens' committee. He worked with us and used us a lot because he didn't have the foot soldiers. On the other hand, we used him. When we wanted to speak to the deputy minister or minister of the environment or other officials, we got the chief to call to arrange meetings. He was persistent, and was almost always successful."

***

What now? Marilyn expressed her doubts. "We are so sceptical," she said. Ian said he is "slightly optimistic" that the BREC notion put forward by Waste Management is just posturing.

He noted that before the Environmental Review Tribunal hearing in the spring of 2015, an official of the company approached Mike Bossio and asked what it would take to settle the issues before the tribunal. "The hearings are expensive," he said. Mike provided them with a list of minimum demands that included the withdrawal of BREC. The company never came back with a response, suggesting that BREC is perhaps just a pawn. But Ian also worried that "the Richmond Landfill rejection sets a terrible example." It shows that Waste Management can be beat, and he thinks they hate losing. For that reason alone, he suggested, they may continue to pursue the BREC environmental assessment.

CHAPTER 17

MISSION ACCOMPLISHED

"If you picked up a copy of the minister's decision . . .
frame it, keep it for the grandchildren."
—lawyer Richard Lindgren, on the environmental
assessment, 2006

Landfill opponents were nervous. The mayor and town councillors were nervous. They were waiting for publication of the "blue book review"—the ministry's review of Waste Management's environmental assessment due April 26, 2006. Timelines were changing; they seemed to have become a moving target. The government review publication date was moved to June 9. The minister's final decision was now due on October 20, 2006.

With ten days left in the public campaign, dump opponents organized a meeting. "We're not done yet. This is not the time to sit back and relax," said Rick Lindgren. "This is a really critical time; between now and next week, we need to give the EA Branch information they need to finally say no to the expansion. We need another tidal wave of public response."[51] And now all they could do was wait out the hours for the government review.

The ministry could put forward one of five recommendations: it could approve the expansion or approve it with conditions; it could deny the expansion; or it could refer the decision to a mediator or to an Environmental Review Tribunal.

On schedule this time, the ministry released the government review on Friday, June 9, 2006. A notice of completion of review posted on the ministry's website stated, "The Review concluded that the EA did not adequately describe existing baseline conditions, meet regulatory requirements for meeting reasonable use limits at the property boundary or provide for a viable leachate control option." The five-hundred-page report concluded that Waste Management had failed to adequately "validate its assumptions and demonstrate that its proposal would not result in any significant adverse effects." The review recommended that "the proposed undertaking not be approved due to the concerns identified by the ministry, members of the Government Review Team, the MBQ and the public."[52]

"Cautiously joyful" was how Steve Medd put it. The residents and the Mohawks felt vindicated. The government review underscored their concerns and the reasons they had been fighting the expansion for nearly a decade. Had they not been lodging complaints with the ministry about contaminants in the water? Had they not been reporting prolonged periods when the stench of rotting garbage hung in the air, sometimes for days and weeks on end? Now, finally, the government reviewers had recognized similar adverse effects.

Hay wagon tour around Richmond Landfill to celebrate negative government review of Waste Management's environmental assessment (June 17, 2006). Photo courtesy of Steve Medd.

"What the ministry's own experts have said, to me, is a complete endorsement of what my clients have been saying for years," said Rick Lindgren. "The community sees [the government review] as good news for the environment." He said the review should set the stage for the outcome of the dump proposal.

The people were aware that the minister could refer the dump proposal to the Environmental Review Tribunal to be decided in a public hearing. For Steve Medd, the possibility of a tribunal hearing meant that it would create "another two years of grief for all the citizens who had been fighting this for the last seven years." He believed there were enough reasons from the government experts to effectively stop the expansion proposal. But he realized the process was not over. "We have to continue our letter-writing campaign. We are gearing up yet again for one more letter to send out."

Rick Lindgren didn't believe there was any need for the case to be heard by the Environmental Review Tribunal. "We know that this site is not approvable and is a very risky undertaking, so in my view there is no need to send it off to the tribunal."

And the waiting continued. Five weeks for public consultation on the government review and thirteen weeks for the minister to review and make a decision. Target date for the minister's decision—October 20, 2006. "The October deadline," said James O'Mara, director of the ministry's Environmental Assessment and Approvals Branch, "is not a hard date." If she felt it was necessary, Minister Laurel Broten could extend the deadline and go beyond the regulated date. Regarding the possible referral of the environmental assessment to the Environmental Review Tribunal, O'Mara said there had not been much history of sending matters to the tribunal.

On October 12, 2006, Waste Management submitted a request to the ministry to withdraw its environmental assessment. Dump opponents saw the eleventh-hour withdrawal as a strategy to gain more time by dragging the process out. The proponent planned to submit a new proposal sometime in January 2007.

The minister's announcement was delayed. The people groaned and patiently waited. Then, on Friday, November 3, 2006, Minister Broten made a surprise announcement. In an eight-page letter to Kevin Bechard, Waste Management, she said that she had decided to refuse the company's request for a hearing, to refuse its request for withdrawal of the environmental assessment, and to refuse to approve this undertaking. "I have determined after careful review that it is in the best interest of public health and the environment to reject this EA proposal," Broten wrote. "The science is clear: this assessment failed to demonstrate that the community's water would be protected."[53]

After battling the proposed landfill expansion for almost a decade, this news was hardly believable. Was it finally over?

Broten referred to the comments received during the public consultation period following the submission of the environmental assessment. "The Ministry received 7,000 submissions opposing the proposed landfill expansion. Together with these submissions, the Ministry also received eleven supplemental technical reports . . . and third party reviews from CELA and other members of the public." Following the completion of the government review, the ministry received over 1,200 comments from the public, which supported the findings of the review and requested that she not refer the application to the Environmental Review Tribunal.

The letter continued: "The First Nations and the public in neighbouring communities brought to light important technical considerations that helped us with our decision. The technical studies that were brought forward indicated the expansion would increase the risk to human health and safety and that it had a high potential to contaminate the local drinking water. That's the basis for the decision."

Rick Lindgren commended the minister for the decision. "It should give other communities fighting landfill expansions hope and confidence as they move forward with their battles," he said. "I think this is very much a David versus Goliath story."[54]

For Allan Gardiner, the news came in a conference call with Minister Broten. "I feel wonderful. It has been a long and hard battle." Nobody knew this better than Allan, who had fought this landfill from the beginning in 1988. "I think the science and technology showed it is an unsafe site." He was already shifting his focus to the closure and ongoing monitoring of the site. "We need to make sure it's done environmentally friendly as far as the closure goes."[55]

Chief Maracle echoed Allan Gardiner's relief at the minister's decision. "I think she has made a very wise choice in terms of protecting the environment for future generations. I personally believe there was potential for a lot of environmental harm to our community from that project." His concern had always been that the site is unsuitable for a landfill.[56]

John Gerretsen, the provincial representative for Kingston and the Islands, agreed it was the right decision. "Hopefully it will put an end to this particular application."[57] Little did he know the role he would play later as environment minister when dump opponents lobbied for its closure.

Officials of Waste Management were surprised and disappointed. "We spent in excess of $7 million and we were at this over eight years. We felt very strongly the EA itself . . . was protective of the environment and the public's health."[58] No one, including the landfill owner, seemed to be clear about how much longer the Richmond Landfill would remain open.

Rick Lindgren wrote to the minister soon after her decision, calling on the ministry to begin the closure process as early as possible.

The existing landfill site is extremely close to reaching capacity and contours under the current certificate of approval. Although the site was still licensed to receive 125,000 tonnes of waste per year, residents living near the site had observed a marked decrease in truck traffic. . . . More importantly, WM's EA itself stated that as of July 2005, the Richmond Landfill had only 1.1 years (130,400 tonnes) of remaining site life. Since more than 15 months have elapsed since this estimate was provided by WM, we can only presume that considerably less capacity (if any) remains today.

He reminded Minister Broten that it was "critical to ensure that effective and enforceable measures are taken to protect local groundwater and surface water resources from adverse effects arising from the closed Richmond Landfill site."[59]

"Let's focus on today." Seven years after beginning the dump fight, Rick Lindgren speaks at a victory celebration after minister's rejection of proposed expansion of the Richmond Landfill (November 19, 2006). Republished with the express permission of *Napanee Guide*, a division of Postmedia Network Inc.

***

About two hundred people gathered on the afternoon of November 19, 2006, at the Mohawk Community Centre for a victory celebration. "There's nothing better than a dump meeting," quipped Allan Gardiner, who could confidently be said to have attended more such meetings than anyone else in the community. The celebration began with a service of thanksgiving led by Chief Don Maracle—thanks were given, hymns were sung, and prayers were said.

After the service came the speeches. Chief Maracle touched on the duty to protect the environment in his speech. "We have to respect the earth . . . we have to think of future generations. This was about our water, this was about our air, this was about respect. We can't be victims of large cities that don't know what to do with their garbage."[60]

It was time to celebrate, Rick Lindgren said. "Let's focus on today." Most of the time, he said, environmental assessments got approved by the minister of the environment. "I was chatting with some of my environmental law colleagues, and we can't recall a single case in recent memory where a minister rejected an environmental assessment. This is significant." Because of the rarity of the decision, he joked, the audience should hold on tight to the copies handed out. "If you picked up a copy of the minister's decision, dated November 3, keep it and cherish it. Frame it, keep it for the grandchildren."[61]

Allan Gardiner graciously thanked members of the community for their hard work and emphasized that it was the collective effort of the residents and the Mohawks of the Bay of Quinte that ultimately produced the victory they would relish for a long, long time. "You should be proud of what you have accomplished."

After the speeches, the crowd was invited to a potluck luncheon. It was here that I first had Mohawk corn soup. And as always at these events, there were Margaret Walsh's cookies and pies.

CHAPTER 18

COMMUNICATE, COMMUNICATE...

*"My motivation...? The usual concerns about the environment, but I am
also deeply offended by the conduct of Waste Management."*
—Jeff Whan, retired IBM executive and anti-dump activist, 2015

In early June 2015, I sat in the sunroom of Jeff and Janet Whan's farm house
on County Road 14, also known as the Croydon Road, due north of Napanee. In the centre of the room, under a heat lamp and inside a low, open
enclosure, were three week-old chicks—Barred Rock hens. They were all
yellow and fluffy, and cheep-cheeping away, but when feathered out they
would don their classic grey/black plumage and become layers of eggs.

In the early 1900s, Croydon boasted several hotels, a general store, a
church, a post office, a schoolhouse, and a gristmill. Not one of those
enterprises exists now, but the Salmon River—the waterway that Steve
Medd is so passionate about—still runs through the heart of Croydon. Jeff
and Janet Whan came to this area in 1976, looking for a weekend gathering place for their seven children in Toronto. If Croydon had seen better
times, so had the house they eventually bought. "The place was a sham-
bles," Jeff said. "The roof was leaking, the basement was flooded, everything was crooked—but we loved it." Jeff is a strapping fellow, just over six
feet tall with a high-beam smile. He radiates intelligence, passion, and
confidence. (When I told Ian Munro that I would be interviewing Jeff
Whan, Ian observed that Jeff brought "gravitas" to the citizens' group.)

Thirteen years ago, when Jeff retired from his job as software executive with IBM, they moved into the Croydon place full-time and began the
serious task of restoring it. The grandson of the previous owner—who lives
across the road—is a carpenter. He was hired to whip the old post-and-
beam clapboard farmhouse into shape. "We kept the footprint," Jeff said.
"We kept the trim." And replaced just about everything else. New floor
joists. Custom windows. Barn restored. Ginger breading replaced.

The property came with a hundred acres and they bought another
hundred across the road to ensure privacy. They filled the place with art
and antiques, and gave it all the attention it had sorely lacked. Now the
flower gardens are splendid. I noticed a good supply of neatly stacked

firewood in an outside open shed. A large rectangular plot was allotted to vegetables, including the asparagus they were to serve for lunch later.

Jeff and Janet (a textile artist who has her own studio in the house) love their country place the way that Mike Bossio loves his old place in Lonsdale. The feeling of these urban transplants for country life goes well beyond convenience and practicality.

"I *am* this place," Jeff told me. These were among the first words he uttered as we settled in the sunroom that day. "This is not our land. We are its custodians. It's true that from where we sit, the Richmond Landfill is well over the horizon in terms of its effect. But I love Napanee. My motivation for being involved in the dump fight? The usual concerns about the environment, but I am also deeply offended by the conduct of Waste Management. I want to expose what I regard as their misdeeds."

Jeff enjoyed a thirty-year career with IBM, working in senior positions in Canada, Europe, and Australia and leading the conversion of that company from one that dealt primarily with hardware into one that started to focus on software. He doesn't buy the claim that all corporations are evil. "When I was at IBM," he told me, "corporate social responsibility was a major part of our agenda." And he is appalled by Waste Management, whose trucks are green and yellow and whose website is emblazoned "Think Green."

Like every person on what he calls "our little citizens' group," Jeff pointed out that working shoulder to shoulder with like-minded people for so long forges deep and abiding friendships. "It's been a privilege," he said. "I admire the whole team. They are now my close friends. We are very fortunate to have found each other and this cause."

And with that, Jeff began to run down the list of his fellow foot soldiers and their attributes. "Steve Medd [the geologist] is brilliant. Ian Munro [a former military man] is one of the smartest people I know. Marilyn Kendall is our 'secret weapon'—a wonderful writer and editor and thinker." He mentioned Wilf Ruland, the hydrogeologist, whose testimony has been so critical. And Rick Lindgren, the tireless Canadian Environmental Law Association lawyer who has fought alongside the citizens' group for many years. He mentioned me—I had apparently familiarized him with some toxicological concepts. As for the Mohawks of the Bay of Quinte and Chief Don Maracle, said Jeff, "We had a high profile at Queen's Park thanks to him."

And Jeff had a lot to say about Mike Bossio. "He is a great leader and enthusiast. He's not always right but he's going a hundred miles an hour. Everyone has to play his or her role for this to work. A volunteer organization is democratic but command and control are essential. A debating society can break out in the middle of a meeting. People want to tell their stories. Mike Bossio pulls us together."

Jeff Whan hosts dinner for friends from the dump fight (August 22, 2014). From top left, Jeff Whan, Chief Don Maracle, Karen Smart, Steve Medd, Dr. John McKinney, Ian Munro, Ed File; from bottom left, Donna Loft, Marilyn Kendall, Mary Lynne Sammon, Margaret Walsh. Photo courtesy of Steve Medd.

I, too, have memories of Mike. How could I forget being at a meeting with Waste Management and some of their macho engineers. They weren't respecting me. Mike stood up and practically blew their heads off, accusing them of being condescending to me—someone he regarded as one of the best toxicologists in the country. I was the only female in the room—and Asian. I was stunned. When he sat down, there was dead silence and everyone was looking down.

As I write this in 2017, Mike Bossio is in Ottawa as a member of Parliament representing Hastings–Lennox and Addington. And not surprisingly, clean water is one of his priorities.

For Jeff, the committee functions so well as a team because each member on the team takes responsibility. "We have had a huge effect," he said. "What we're achieving is a model for others. Everyone participates according to his or her ability and expertise. Mine is communication."

Jeff remembers entering the fray during the early days, in 2004. Steve Medd had written one of his many incendiary letters to the *Napanee Beaver*, and a meeting was called. Don Ryan and Allan Gardiner, two stalwarts of the battle in those years, got into what Jeff calls "a huge fight." There was tension in the group as any new members were looked upon as possible spies for Waste Management. Later, Don Ryan called Jeff Whan. "We can beat these buggers," Don told Jeff. Jeff agreed but what was lacking, in his estimation, was a communications strategy.

Each according to their expertise, indeed.

Communications was Jeff Whan's bread and butter. He developed a communications plan—a veritable book. Who the audience was for citizens' group communications, how to present to each one. Jeff saw that the Mohawks, the concerned citizens' committee, and the Town of Napanee each had their own agenda.

A communications committee was formed, with Jeff as its chair. They met once a week and started to lobby local and provincial politicians. "We spent," said Jeff, "an enormous amount of time communicating with politicians. We met the premier, we cultivated our own relationships. We got audiences thanks to Leona Dombrowsky [the local representative from 2003 to 2011 and minister of the environment from 2003 to 2005]." All that work paid off.

In 2006, the province's minister of the environment rejected the environmental assessment on the proposed dump expansion and it seemed as if the dump fight had finally been won. Jeff remembered meeting with ministry officials and how he and his fellow committee members felt welcome. "We had cultivated a pretty good relationship," Jeff said. "We felt they were cheering for us. I don't feel that way now."

The elation of 2006 quickly evaporated. A new proposed landfill—Beechwood Road Environmental Centre—was put forward by Waste Management, and for Jeff and his colleagues it looked a lot like the previous one. And right next to the old site. How, the committee asked, could the ministry possibly entertain this new project when one just like it had been so soundly rejected? Shockingly, the ministry had approved the terms of reference of the environmental assessment for this project. They had just rejected the environmental assessment for Waste Management's proposed landfill expansion, citing environmental and health reasons. It was as though we were starting anew and had never gone through the first process.

Whatever naïveté Jeff Whan once possessed about the stewardship role of government has been quashed. "I have come to understand," he once told me, "that we cannot count on the Ontario government to protect the environment. I want the government to reset their priorities from polluting industry enablers to stewards of sustainability. I want to show what can be done, and to model the way for other communities facing similar ill-conceived proposals."

Jeff blames the process—"the cumbersome, flawed mechanism"—by which such decisions are made. The process, he argues, is not based on environmental grounds but political ones.

"We set the record for the number of letters sent. We met with the deciders, the politicians. We used the *Environmental Bill of Rights* a number of times. We celebrated when the environmental assessment for the proposed landfill expansion was rejected. We thought then that our fight was over. Not so. We ended up fighting for closure. Now we're at the Environmental Review Tribunal for safe closure conditions and monitoring. But ultimately, this is all political. We hope the minister of the environment makes the decision based on science. And I do believe they have a system based on science."

However, Jeff knows well that the minister is the ultimate decision-maker. And the long history of the Richmond Landfill is littered with decisions that defy all sense. The approval of the terms of reference of the environmental assessment for the BREC, for one. A second bad decision concerned the *Environmental Bill of Rights* application that the citizens' committee and the Mohawks submitted in 2013. It requested that the Ministry of the Environment review and amend the *Environmental Protection Act* (EPA) to prohibit new or expanded waste disposal sites at hydrogeologically unsuitable locations. Based on their knowledge and experience with the Richmond Landfill, the application also requested that the Act be amended to prohibit proponents from resubmitting proposals that had previously been rejected due to the unsuitability of the site. The Ministry of the Environment denied the request both to review and to make amendments. It missed an opportunity to fix a widespread problem, that of appropriate and safe siting for waste disposal sites.

In the meantime, the process is heavily weighted in the developer's favour—and not least because the lack of intervenor funding makes it easy for a large landfill company to outgun and outspend a little citizens' group trying to muster funds through bake sales.

"We have advocated changing the process," Jeff told me. "Rick Lindgren has been involved in a review panel convened by the provincial Liberal government of Dalton McGuinty, and they have produced a two-volume report suggesting critical changes to improve the process. That was in 2005 and nothing has happened. I am not holding my breath waiting for anything to happen now." In an ideal world, said Jeff, the Environmental Review Tribunal would order costs—meaning that if the developer loses the fight, it pays the citizens' costs. That said, it is in all likelihood not a viable option, since it is not easy in tribunal proceedings to identify winners and losers.

Often, an appellant wins on some issues and loses on others.

Jeff strikes me as a generally upbeat and optimistic man, but his frustration showed as he talked about both the Ministry of the Environment and the waste company.

"There are some good people at the MOE," he said. "Kyle Stephenson, their hydrogeologist, is a good guy. He identified the plume of leachate migrating out of the landfill boundary. But the MOE sees their job as facilitating industry. Why won't the MOE enforce the notification protocols? Our little citizens' group is doing the job that the Ministry of the Environment should be doing. Waste Management does not communicate and the Ministry of the Environment does not force them to. As for Waste Management, why don't they do the right thing? It's in their interests to do the right thing, but no, they do the *opposite* of what you think. Every PR handbook says you should communicate, express concern and respond to outrage. They deny and deny, they drag their feet. The plume was detected years ago. No response from the company. All they see is a two-billion-dollar business opportunity. This style of corporate behaviour must not be rewarded."

Jeff wished the dump battle would just end and that Waste Management would retreat with its tail between its legs, but he could not see that happening. "I think this thing will just keep on going. There's no end in sight. Just listen to the company's rhetoric: 'We have a monitoring plan . . . We have a good location.' Their history is they never pull out. They are dogged."

The citizens' group, meanwhile, is aging, and while there is some new blood on the committee, will that be enough? How long can they keep on raising money? For Jeff, one of the biggest questions is this one: Who is going to replace Mike Bossio now that he has been elected and is in Ottawa?

"Meanwhile," said Jeff, "the bloody thing is still leaking." The citizens' group has a website, of course. It's called LeakyLand. A group of dump opponents was having discussions about what to call their new site. They came up with the name "Leaky Landfill," but thought that might not be appropriate as there was no solid evidence at the time that the landfill was leaking leachate off-site. They shortened it, and that's how LeakyLand was born.

In a way, Jeff was feeling trapped. "I can't get out," he said. "I possess a body of knowledge about the science on dumps and how the game is played. In the meantime, all the Waste Management and Ministry of the Environment people have changed. We are the same but on the other side there is no institutional memory of what happened."

Jeff hopes that a benefactor will come along, someone with deep pockets and a passion for the environment. He worries that climate change is getting all the press while water—that precious resource—is not a priority. "It's totally wrong," he said, "that a political decision will decide this matter when a plume is heading for Lake Ontario."

Jeff Whan took a deep breath. "We will never give up."

He offered this advice for anyone pitted against unwanted development. "You can affect the outcome. Get engaged. Figure out the process. Find out who makes the decisions and what influences them. Always be professional. Get your facts right. Walk a mile in the shoes of your opposition. Is there compromise or accommodation? If not, where are they vulnerable? Communicate, communicate. Figure out your assets. Who has what background? Get everyone working from a point of strength and form a team."

More often than not, anyone intent on taking on a corporation has to realize that the odds are stacked against them. On the other hand, I well remember Rick Lindgren talking about his experience of the dump fight, which has occupied him since 1999. "Could you ever work for a corporate client, as some lawyers do—sometimes acting for the big guys, sometimes for the little guys, sometimes for the good guys, sometimes for the bad guys?" I asked. He replied, "I could never work for a big company or a bad company. I just love the people."

**

"Communicate, communicate," was Jeff's mantra. One person I wanted to interview was not affiliated with the waste company, the government, or the citizens' group but reported on all three: Seth DuChene, editor of the *Napanee Beaver*. Seth is a forty-five-year-old father of two, a sixteen-year-old boy and a seven-year-old girl. His wife, Mary Beth, is a teacher, Napanee born and bred, and he grew up near the village of Tamworth, north of Napanee. He is, in other words, local, and he understands the town very well. One Friday morning, just a week after I had chatted with Jeff Whan, I met Seth at the newspaper's office on Dundas Street for a chat. Seth was wearing a golf shirt, shorts, and running shoes with green laces, clothing that seemed to match his laid-back nature. The *Beaver* office was closed on Friday, so it was his day off work.

Were you not working for the newspaper, I asked him, would you have been an anti-dump activist?

"No," he replied, easing into a grin. "I'm not that guy."

Seth started covering the dump fight when the first rumblings began, in 1998. He had just been hired two years before as a reporter at the paper. By 2001 he was the editor. No surprise, after seventeen years, he is weary of the dump story. Some years ago he was more than happy to hand off the dump file to one of his reporters. "The longer the fight went on," Seth observed, "people in town tuned it out. I got that sense."

I could not help but wonder if Seth himself had tuned it out. For one thing, the anger of dump detractors repelled him. "People were so passionate," he said, "and I was so dispassionate. I don't like meetings where people yell and scream. I did not like being there. It wore me down. I liked the people opposed but I dreaded talking to them. They expected me to be on side."

At one point in our conversation, Seth said some things that surprised me. "I look at the other side," he told me. "The company seems to be playing by the rules and going through the environment ministry's hoops. If the experts say it's safe, maybe it is. Money talks. Part of me has a hard time believing that people would be that careless. I also believe, and I wrote editorials about this, that with all the cutbacks, the Ministry of the Environment could not do due diligence. But my underlying assumption is that the Ministry of the Environment would not allow an unsafe site to proceed."

I'm more cynical than that. If a government ministry is compromised by cutbacks, is it actually in a position to declare a site safe, or not?

Then Seth seemed to contradict what he had just said—or maybe he had just given the other side its due, and was now turning to my side. "Opponents of the landfill talk about fractured limestone," he went on, "and so many experts say it's not a good place for a landfill. They had a strong case. It was not a frivolous complaint."

Seth DuChene is a fine writer. I wondered aloud why he stayed in Napanee when it was apparent that his talent could have taken him to a bigger publication in a bigger place. But he has deep roots here in a town that has not changed all that much in decades.

"There are more stores, more activity," he said, "but the essential character has not changed. There are lots of things I could grumble about and a lot of things I like. It's a small town. People here are small-c conservative."

But that's what made the dump story so irresistible to Seth DuChene and the *Napanee Beaver*. All those sparks flying at meetings and in letters to the editor, more than eight thousand protest letters sent, a mind-boggling quarter of a million dollars raised by a small band of people. "Unprecedented," commented Seth.

I wished that Jeff Whan had been in the boardroom of the *Beaver* that day to hear Seth's prediction on the fate of the dump. "I don't see that site being used," Seth said. "They're trying to fit a square peg into a round hole. It's already failed once. Now there's an Environmental Review Tribunal. In my heart of hearts, I can't see it going ahead. If it were to go ahead,

I would be shocked." He also observed that Waste Management had a presence in the community in past years. "I don't see that happening so much now."

Seth wrote many fiercely smart editorials on the landfill and raised hard questions. He had also been extremely kind to me and generous with his time when I wanted to search in the basement of the *Beaver* for old stories as part of my research. I called that basement "the catacombs"; it's a wonderful cache of hardbound-by-year *Beavers* that date back to the late 1800s, when the paper was founded. When I had to find stories down there, Seth would guide me to them or find the correct issues for me. One day, we were down in the catacombs looking for a number of back issues. We could not find them readily, and Seth was going through the piles of papers. Soon dust was floating in the air from the old newsprint. Undeterred, Seth lifted his T-shirt and covered his nose, and soon found what I was looking for. My gratitude for his efforts that day could not be greater.

Seth DuChene has a place in this story not because I consider him an ally to the cause, but because the newspaper he edited was so vigilant and attentive on the landfill issue. And the writing was several notches above what might have been expected for a small-town paper. Seth did his homework before writing his editorials. I watched him at the Environmental Review Tribunal hearing in Belleville in the spring of 2015, his computer open at his lap, his focus intense on the witnesses, his fingers flying.

If indeed the battle has been won, at least some credit should go to a small-town journalist. Indifferent and dispassionate though he may have sounded in our conversation, I think part of that is the man's own nature and another part is a small-town survival tactic. The editor of the local paper can't be seen to belong to any one camp, and he keeps his editorial distance. But his dispatches on the dump story played no small part in keeping the issue alive.

CHAPTER 19

JUDGMENT DAYS: THE ENVIRONMENTAL REVIEW TRIBUNAL

"I have never been involved in a hearing such as this.
There are so many questions with no answers."
—lawyer Richard Lindgren at the Environmental
Review Tribunal, June 2015

In an old western, the cowboy accused of cattle rustling or bank robbing would be parked in a sheriff's jail cell until the judge arrived in town to hear his case. These were circuit judges, and they would make their rounds, conduct their trials, and then move on to the next dusty town. There were no courthouses, so ad hoc courtrooms were set up in a saloon or sheriff's office or hotel.

I was reminded of those scenes of the Wild West when, in April through June, 2015, the Environmental Review Tribunal made stops in the Greater Napanee area to weigh in yet again on the matter of Waste Management of Canada versus citizens' groups opposed to the Richmond Landfill. The ERT member, Maureen Carter-Whitney, had also come around the year before. Why? In a nutshell, the citizens' group, the CCCTE, and their lawyer, Rick Lindgren, had objected to some of the conditions governing closure of the landfill. The Ministry of the Environment and Climate Change had simply accepted the conditions of the landfill closure plan set down by the company, and on January 16, 2012, the ministry issued a document (formally called Amended Environmental Compliance Approval) that defined conditions for the closure plan, including monitoring and mitigating the potential environmental impacts of the closed landfill. Rick and the concerned citizens' committee agreed: this was like putting the fox in charge of the henhouse. They took issue with seven conditions in the approval document governing monitoring programs, contingency plans, and reporting.

On January 30, 2012, Rick Lindgren, on behalf of the CCCTE, submitted an application under the *Environmental Bill of Rights* for leave to appeal the seven conditions. Rick argued that the ministry's approval was "substantively deficient, procedurally flawed, and unlikely to provide timely and effective protection of the environment." The tribunal—and this was rare—granted leave to appeal all seven conditions. Over the course of two years, agreement on three of the seven conditions was negotiated, but mediation failed to yield consensus on the remaining four—to be decided by the tribunal in a public hearing.

Just like in the movies, the tribunal featured many accoutrements of a genuine court. "All rise," someone would say when the ERT member walked in or exited. Carter-Whitney would take her seat and then invite everyone else to do the same. She took copious notes, and I often wondered how she was able to make sense of the enormously complex legal file of an environmental battle that had endured for decades.

Carter-Whitney struck me by her courtesy, her keen intelligence, the way she gave no clue to her thinking. I looked up her background. She formerly worked as research director for the Canadian Institute for Environmental Law and Policy; she has been a legal analyst for the environmental commissioner of Ontario and a course instructor in environmental law at Ryerson University. She holds a Bachelor of Arts degree from the University of Toronto, a Bachelor of Laws degree from the University of British Columbia, and a Master of Laws degree from Osgoode Hall Law School. Solid credentials, to be sure.

There was a certain formality to the hearing. Witnesses and experts were called to the stand (which was a chair and table to the ERT member's right), to be probed by lawyers friendly and lawyers hostile and sometimes by the ERT member herself. Oversized maps were displayed at the front of the room, and for week after week, the Richmond Landfill was explored in picayune detail before forty or so onlookers who often included many of the citizens I've profiled. The venues, a hotel in Belleville and a community centre in Tyendinaga Township, lent a certain air of informality to proceedings. No wigged lawyers here, just men and women in suits. At the community centre, I noticed, white chiffon ribbons hung from the ceiling, a remnant, I presumed, of a wedding reception.

By the summer of 2011, the dump had been officially closed. At issue now were the terms of closure. How often should groundwater and surface water in and around the dump be tested? How precisely and promptly should citizens be notified of test results, particularly when they indicated negative impacts? What contingency plans were in place? This was an important consideration, since leachate might continue to emanate from the dumpsite for a century or more—whether the company was around that long or not. Finally—and this is where my testimony as a toxicologist would come to the fore—what leachate constituents and what levels of those constituents were permissible?

Especially contentious was a particular chemical commonly found in leachate: 1,4-dioxane, regarded as the best leachate marker and one classified by some regulatory agencies as a probable human carcinogen. The issue had become complicated because there was neither a provincial nor a federal drinking water standard for 1,4-dioxane. Therefore, a drinking water standard had to be set for use at this site. A lot rode on this standard, for the proponent and for the local communities.

Negotiations involving the waste company, the provincial Ministry of the Environment and Climate Change, and the citizens' groups had to this point not yielded a compromise on what constituted a safe level for this chemical toxicant. I had recommended a drinking water standard for 1,4-dioxane of 3.0 micrograms per litre. The ministry recommended a standard of 30.0 micrograms per litre, and Waste Management—after initially pushing for a standard of 350 micrograms per litre—now agreed with that standard, but with qualification. We had all dug our heels in, and this was the situation when we headed for the hearing.

A drinking water standard for the vicinity of the Richmond Landfill had become critical, as by now leachate had been identified outside the landfill boundaries. Provincial regulations stipulated that water emanating from a contaminated site was allowable provided the level did not exceed 25 per cent of the drinking water standard. This was referred to as the Reasonable Use Limit. Accordingly, the Reasonable Use Limit calculated from my recommended standard would be 0.75 micrograms per litre (due to technical limitations, rounded to 1.0 microgram per litre). The ministry's Reasonable Use Limit would be 7.5 micrograms per litre. On the other hand, Waste Management put forward a "compliance limit" of 30 micrograms per litre, and asserted that this value be used instead of calculating a Reasonable Use Limit. ("Compliance limit," by the way, is not a term in the regulatory lexicon or in normal use.) What was behind this unusual strategy? No doubt, in my view, it was to limit the money that would have to be spent on compliance with a more stringent regulatory standard.

The Environmental Review Tribunal hearing involved a long, protracted process, and a lot depended on the 1,4-dioxane drinking water standard—not only for drinking water but also for remediating contaminated land. An accepted approach for the latter is for the landfill owner to establish a Contaminant Attenuation Zone on affected lands where the contaminants are allowed to deteriorate naturally over time. This, of course, assumes that the landfill owner will acquire the properties if it does not already own them. How the boundaries of this Contaminant Attenuation Zone are delineated will depend largely on the drinking water standard.

Rick Lindgren, acting for the concerned citizens, put it well one day in June 2015 when he said at the tribunal hearing, "I have never been involved in a hearing such as this. There are so many questions with no answers." But the bottom line was this: "We have a leaky landfill that needs to be fixed."

***

One measure of the complexity of the landfill issue was the document-heavy accordion-style satchel and numerous boxes that Rick Lindgren had to schlep into the courtroom, wherever it might be. That always involved several trips. Eric Gillespie, the lawyer acting for the Mohawks of the Bay of Quinte, had a junior lawyer to help lug his boxes. Waste Management's lead lawyer, Harry Dahme, was likewise burdened. The Ministry of the Environment had its own lawyer, Paul McCulloch, plus help, at the tribunal hearing. Also there was a young lawyer, Ian Miron, for Napanee Green Lights, an informal environmental group headed by a family doctor in Napanee, Tom Touzel. An avid environmentalist (he lives with his family in an off-grid nineteenth-century log house on the Napanee River), Dr. Touzel cycled to the hearing one day wearing a pointedly green T-shirt.

Witnesses to the tribunal hearing offer first a written statement that outlines their background, relevant credentials, and point of view. Before I was called to the witness stand, for example, I had worked with Rick Lindgren on the best way to make my points, on what to expect as a challenge from the Waste Management lawyer, and so on. I am a confident person and well schooled in my area of expertise, but still, it's unnerving to be on the hot spot. Sleep never came easy on the night before my testimony. I was calm but wired.

During those small hours, I had ample time to think of my ten-year-long involvement in this struggle. I am now a retired professor from Queen's University, but was still teaching and doing research when I started working with Rick Lindgren. Did I regret all that time spent on this front? Absolutely not. I wanted to link arms with people I had worked with closely and look back on all our hard work as part of our legacy. I had once asked Ian Munro why he spent so much of his life on this project. His response: "Because it makes a difference, because it makes the world a better place." I pondered that for a long while. Perhaps it was a bit like that for me.

***

My witness statement read, in part:

> I am a scientist with over 30 years experience in research, publishing, reviewing, and consulting in the field of chemical

toxicology. In particular, my research activities have focused on mechanisms that mediate toxicities produced by environmental chemicals. I have published over 80 papers and book chapters in established peer-reviewed journals and books in the field of Pharmacology and Toxicology. The research in my laboratory has been funded by agencies including Canadian Institutes of Health Research, National Cancer Institute of Canada, U.S. National Institutes of Health, U.S. Environmental Protection Agency and others. I have been involved in health risk assessments for the U.S. Environmental Protection Agency, Health Canada, Environment Canada, and others.

I had also taught anatomy at Queen's University and lectured in toxicology. I take a biological and biochemical approach when it comes to the impact of toxic chemicals on human health. I want to know: Why was the cell damaged? What's the reason for a toxic response? How can the negative response be prevented or reversed?

The CCCTE and its lawyer had asked me to weigh in on the subject of 1,4-dioxane, a chemical I had been looking at closely since 2013. On April 17, 2015, at the Travelodge Hotel in Belleville, and in response to questions—first from Rick Lindgren and then from Harry Dahme and Paul McCulloch—I told the tribunal what I had learned about 1,4-dioxane.

There are many problems with this so-called heterocyclic organic compound, starting with its prevalence and persistence in the environment. This probable human carcinogen and tumour promoter is used in cosmetics, textiles, printing, paints, contraceptives, condoms, pesticides, anti-freeze, solvents—and even to purify drugs. We are all exposed to 1,4-dioxane on a daily basis. Worse, this chemical mixes well with water, is highly mobile, does not bind to soil particles or biodegrade, and can rapidly migrate in groundwater ahead of other contaminants.

Because 1,4-dioxane is so widespread, I told the tribunal, we should take a precautionary approach and keep permissible levels of this chemical in drinking water as low as possible, especially for vulnerable groups such as children. I had read all available literature and examined animal studies as well as various state regulations in the United States, where this compound has been extensively studied. Based on the cumulative data, I recommended a Reasonable Use Limit of 1.0 microgram per litre. The Ministry of the Environment and Climate Change proposed a Reasonable Use Limit of 7.5 micrograms per litre, while Waste Management was pushing for what it called a compliance limit of 30 micrograms per litre.

The issue of what level of 1,4-dioxane would be selected marked one of the few times during the three-week-long tribunal hearing that things got testy. The landfill company's lawyer, Harry Dahme, bristled when I suggested during my testimony that "we are only dealing with one carcinogen. There is more than one."

"There is no evidence of any other carcinogen, in the case of this landfill," the lawyer told me.

I replied, "We don't test for a lot of chemicals, so I would say that there is no evidence either for the chemicals you haven't tested for."

"You are speculating," Dahme shot back.

"And so are you," I countered.

At one point, I answered his question with a question. He responded, "I am not under cross-examination. You are." I smiled, finding this exchange rather amusing.

Later in my testimony, he scolded me yet again. "*Don't* speculate," he barked, prompting Rick Lindgren to intervene. "We don't need," he told the ERT member, "that kind of admonition from my friend."

For the record: When the hydrogeologist for the concerned citizens, Wilf Ruland, took the stand, he described the chemical composition of the leachate from the landfill, noting that leachate from municipal waste typically contains thousands of chemicals. He further described landfill leachate as a noxious, toxic liquid. The chemical load in the leachate will eventually drop to a point where it is no longer of consequence, but no one can say with any certainty when that will be.

***

Over the course of nineteen days in 2015, witness after witness was called to testify at the tribunal. Mike Bossio, Ian Munro, Chief Don Maracle, hydrogeologists and engineers from both sides, the director of the Ministry of the Environment and Climate Change, and a great many others. Boxes were lugged in and out of venues, notes were taken, witnesses grilled. What a task it must have been for the ERT member to summarize every witness statement and then to rule on whose testimony made the most sense. Having sat through the testimony of most of the witnesses, I would say that the material presented by the several hydrogeologists was the most challenging. I soon lost track of how many monitoring wells there were, where they were located, and what levels of chemicals were detected. At one point, I asked Rick if he thought Carter-Whitney would read all those boxes of documents. He said yes, and as it turned out, he was correct. She did.

On December 24, 2015, Maureen Carter-Whitney released her 159-page ruling. Case number 12-033, the document was labelled. It was more than I had dared hope for. The citizens got almost everything they asked for, and the landfill company did not win a single significant concession. The Reasonable Use Limit for 1,4-dioxane in drinking water for example, was set at 1.0 microgram per litre. Indeed, the ERT member pointedly dismissed the Waste Management toxicologist who had argued for a limit hundreds of times higher than that. "The Tribunal," wrote Carter-Whitney, "does not find Dr. [Michael] Dourson's recommendation to be of assistance. His opinion is based on a recent re-interpretation of a study, has received limited peer review and not yet received agency or public review." Ouch.

The tribunal also set a Reasonable Use Limit of 1.0 microgram per litre for the boundaries of the Contamination Attenuation Zone, and to expand the boundaries in the future, if needed. It ordered the landfill owner to carry out additional investigations to address the extent of leachate contamination. Only when the leachate plume has been delineated can the boundaries of the Contamination Attenuation Zone be established.

On the day after Christmas 2015, when almost everyone on the CCCTE had had a chance to digest the tribunal's final decision and orders, emails flew among us. The general sense was jubilation.

Ian Munro sent out this email:

Boy, go away for twenty-four hours and, bang, Santa delivers this gem! A 1,4-dioxane limit of 1 microgram per liter—excellent. Acknowledgement of widespread off-site contamination (as compared to total denial of ANY impacts). Waste Management spending millions of dollars on wells and testing with the prospect that they will need to spend millions more. A Ministry of the Environment and Climate Change (MOECC) that has been shown to have failed in its duties to protect local citizens and the environment over many years. And possibly the most important development is the confirmation of the lie that this site can be safely and effectively monitored by a company with significant financial vested interest and an MOECC with limited resources (and apparently little incentive) to hold them accountable. Many thanks to Rick, Wilf, Poh-Gek and all the volunteers who got us through the process.

Wilf Ruland wrote in his email, "Wow! Lots of gifts! This sure counts as a victory to be celebrated in my opinion. The Tribunal has accepted the majority of our evidence, and worded its decision accordingly." He was very pleased with the 1 microgram per litre ruling on 1,4-dioxane and pleased, too, that almost all of his recommendations to do with the frequency and degree of monitoring had been endorsed.

The only "coal" that Wilf could see was that the tribunal had punted the amendments for the Environmental Compliance Approval back to the ministry's director to adjudicate the warring factions—citizens, ministry, and industry—on the amendments. Remember, this was the official responsible for starting the ball rolling towards the tribunal, so there wasn't much trust that he'd get it right. In the end, Carter-Whitney would have to step in to settle the final wording of the document.

Ian Munro later drafted a press release that quoted Rick Lindgren. "The Environmental Review Tribunal decision," the lawyer said, "wholly vindicates my client's long-standing concerns about groundwater contamination emanating from the Richmond Landfill Site. In addition, it is my view that the Tribunal's findings make it abundantly clear that this fractured bedrock setting is unsuitable for the massive Beechwood Road Environmental Centre (BREC) landfill being proposed by Waste Management beside the Richmond Landfill."

Importantly, the tribunal's decision confirmed that Waste Management was responsible for the massive off-site contamination caused by the Richmond Landfill, and for the very challenging task of trying to track the off-site contamination in the complex and highly unpredictable groundwater flow system.

Ian Munro, the new chair of CCCTE, reflected on the group's efforts and accomplishments. "It was a long and (at times) tedious road but ultimately the ERT appeal process did dramatically advance our attempts to protect local communities from the impacts of the Richmond Landfill."

I had learned a great deal from my involvement in the Richmond Landfill saga, including this indisputable fact: garbage can come back to haunt us. In this case, with leachate currently migrating in unknown directions outside the landfill site. The unfinished business was delineation of the leachate plume. And defining the boundaries of the Contaminant Attenuation Zone, which could only be accomplished when the leachate plume has been delineated. In July 2016, the parties met with the ministry for an update. Based on the data provided by the company, the ministry concluded that "the delineation of off-site leachate impacted groundwater and surface water has not been completed." It advised Waste Management that it was required to undertake additional work and submit a report by December 30, 2016. December came and went, and no report appeared. I inquired and was told another extension had been granted. Ian Munro opined that this is a familiar storyline that will keep on being repeated. And so we wait. It is evident that water quality issues remain very much alive, and Ian wonders whether they will be resolved in our lifetimes. A depressing thought.

***

On October 26, 2016, Environmental Commissioner of Ontario Dianne Saxe released a two-volume 2015/1016 Environmental Protection Report, *Small Steps Forward*. In volume 1, the commissioner highlighted the case of the Richmond Landfill, together with the tribunal hearing and decision, as an example of the successful use of third-party appeal rights under the *Environmental Bill of Rights* to improve environmental protection. The dump activists read the report and felt gratified. The good guys won this one.

***

I ran into Barbara Linds, CCCTE member Eric DePoe's partner, at a local coffee shop.

She said, "I hear that you all won at the tribunal hearing."

"Yeah, big time."

"You should have a celebration. At our restaurant." Barbara and Eric are proprietors of the Waterfall Tearoom at Yarker, a small village north of Kingston on the Napanee River.

I was puzzled. "But you have closed your restaurant." Chef Eric had said to me on my last visit to the restaurant, "I am in my sixties and cooking is a young man's game."

"We can open it again for one day," Barbara replied.

I relayed this information to Ian Munro, who thought it a great idea. Jeff Whan and Carolyn Butts dove in to do the organizing.

So we had a victory party the evening of April 29, 2016. When I entered the restaurant with Chief Don Maracle, there was Eric in his chef's garb. Steve Medd and his buddies supplied the music—a trio of guitar, mandolin, and drum. I did a double take—the guy with the mandolin was my egg man at the Kingston farmer's market. And later, Steve Medd teamed up with Mohawk musician David Maracle. Before long, the place was packed with people, many familiar faces but also many I had never seen before. Trays of food circulated, featuring finger food cooked by an Ojibwe chef—smoked duck and sweetgrass, elk sliders, mushrooms with sumac. I never knew that game and foraged foods could taste so good.

Carolyn informed me that this was an event for both local folks and Mohawks. After all, they had waged the landfill fight together and it was only fitting that they celebrate together. The event was dubbed Raise a Glass to Water. Wilf Ruland drove for three hours to attend. He planned to stay the night at Ian Munro's place, and take a "walkabout" at the Richmond Landfill site the next morning before driving home. I was glad to see him—we had worked well together at the tribunal hearing, and we congratulated each other.

The evening began with a Mohawk water ceremony, one that involves only women. Betty Maracle, a middle-aged Mohawk woman, had in front of her a wooden bucket containing water from the Napanee River and a basket. Holding an eagle feather, she spoke about the streams and rivers, and how the Mohawk people called them the veins of Mother Earth. She said that when Mohawk people wake up in the morning, they thank Mother Earth for the trees, the streams, the sun, the birds, and the beauty of nature. (I was standing next to Don and asked him whether he did that each morning. "Of course," he replied.) She then took some tobacco out of the basket and spoke about its special role in Mohawk culture. At the end of the evening, the tobacco was scattered into the water. While David Maracle played the flute, Betty and Kimberly Maracle, another Mohawk woman, took the bucket outside and emptied it over the bridge into the river. And so the water is returned to its source. For many, it was a highlight of the evening.

I thought it a highly successful event. Ian agreed. "Much awareness building and some general goodwill promoted, and we got donations totalling five hundred dollars without really trying." Fundraising remained a persistent problem for CCCTE. That evening Ian had announced that the car parked outside the restaurant, a 1985 Datsun 300zx, was for sale. He was the original owner and had maintained it with his considerable mechanical skills. He tried to convince me that I would look good in it. It was sold a few weeks later to a collector for five thousand dollars, which Ian donated to the dump fund.

Late that night, Don sent me an email message, "It was a lovely event." On that score, we could all agree.

***

In the story of David versus Goliath, a boy-man slays a giant and well-armed soldier using only a sling and a stone. Then David cuts off Goliath's head, using the latter's own sword.

The dump saga has often been compared to that parable, and I confess to liking the comparison. The problem is that this modern-day Goliath seems to come back from the dead. The tribunal's findings offered us hope, for good sense had prevailed. But why was another dump even on the table—when the old one next door had so many problems and had been so roundly rejected? Waste Management has spent a small fortune on that landfill site, and those of us on the concerned citizens' committee could not agree: Was all that money spent reason to now abandon this project, or reason to stay in the game?

In 2010, after the original dump expansion was rejected, Waste Management submitted a proposal to build the Beechwood Road Environmental Centre—a recycling centre alongside a new landfill site that would accept 400,000 tonnes of waste per year over a span of twenty years. The rejection of the original environmental assessment for the Richmond site expansion marked only the second time such an assessment had been rejected in Ontario. Never before had a proponent been rejected before coming back to the table with another proposal for the same site. It boggles the mind.

Rick Lindgren has a gift for metaphor. "If they want to keep that train wreck in motion," he once said, referring to the BREC, "that's their choice. I put them on notice that we intend to drop the gloves and we'll pummel the documents until we get the result we're looking for, which is another rejection of the same dumb landfilling idea at the same dumb site."[62]

Seth DuChene, in a July 18, 2013, editorial in the *Beaver*, nicely captured the absurdity of the company reviving a moribund idea:

[Waste Management] says that it can "understand" the complex geology underneath the site, and that its state-of-the-art liner and leachate collection systems will ensure their landfill won't impact the surrounding environment per stringent MOE specifications; meanwhile, the opponents contend that the site is fundamentally unsuitable for a landfill because no liner system is foolproof, and failure . . . will cause contamination of groundwater that is difficult, if not impossible, to remediate. Further, having made that argument successfully once, it shouldn't have to be made again.

As I was writing this book, I would often end a chapter with "To be continued . . ." And as I come to the end in early 2017, I have to ask myself: When will I stop asking what's next? When will the Richmond Landfill saga ever end?

CHAPTER 20

LESSONS LEARNED

In time, almost everyone in the community knew why the geology of the site made it unsuitable for garbage disposal.

At the same time that the concerned citizens' group was fighting the proposed landfill expansion at Richmond, Waste Management was pitching landfill expansion proposals at Warwick Landfill in Lambton County in southwestern Ontario and Carp Road Landfill in Ottawa. The environmental assessment for the proposed expansion of the Warwick Landfill, located in the Township of Warwick, was approved by the Ministry of the Environment in January 2007. The approval would allow the proponent to receive 750,000 tonnes of waste from Ontario for a period of approximately twenty-five years.[63] The Carp Landfill, now called the West Carleton Environmental Centre and located in the City of Ottawa, had its environmental assessment approved in August 2013. The annual disposal rate was estimated to be 400,000 tonnes per year of waste from Ontario, with an additional 150,000 tonnes per year of daily cover. The estimated site life was approximately ten years.[64]

Citizens' groups in both places vigorously opposed the expansions, but failed to stop them. How did dump opponents in Greater Napanee and the Tyendinaga Mohawk Territory achieve the unexpected end result? What are the lessons to be learned from "fighting dirty" at the Richmond Landfill?

The answers lie, in part, at the beginning. When local citizens began their fight, they had no strategies other than those based on instinct and common sense. It wasn't until 1999, when Rick Lindgren got involved, that they starting receiving guidance based on environmental law and provincial regulations. The citizens' group was poor enough to access provincial legal aid. With a skilled environmental lawyer on their side, the opposition now gained direction and focus, and a strategic plan of action for the fight.

Rick has worked closely with the citizens' group for almost two decades. He carried them through two court cases—a judicial review and an appeal—and an environmental assessment process. In the spring of 2015, he led them through a public hearing held by the Environmental Review Tribunal regarding the terms of closure at the Richmond Landfill site. This took place over nineteen days from April 13 to June 22, 2015.

At the hearing, CCCTE was the appellant—it initiated the appeal—and the respondents were the director, Ministry of the Environment, and Waste Management of Canada Corporation. The Mohawks of the Bay of Quinte and Napanee Green Lights were parties to the appeal. The tribunal ruled in favour of the citizens' groups, and orders were issued for stricter monitoring of the closed waste site and more extensive investigation of a leachate plume migrating off-site. Without a doubt, an environmental lawyer is a must for citizen opponents to manoeuvre through the minefield of provincial regulations. CCCTE members believe that if Lindgren had not become involved, they would likely be living today next to a mega-dump. They are still horrified at how close this scenario came to being a reality.

Rick Lindgren needed experts for their technical knowledge. Hydrogeologist Wilf Ruland understood the dynamics of groundwater and surface water. I provided information on chemical exposures through landfill gas and contaminated water, and carried out health risk assessments. The Mohawks of the Bay of Quinte retained me to assess the health impacts of the landfill. They also retained Kevin Shipley of XCG Consultants Ltd., and Neegan Burnside, a majority-owned aboriginal engineering firm that works with First Nations, to study the geology and hydrogeology in the vicinity of the site. All of this consultation was an expensive proposition, but it is imperative that experts are retained to address the technical aspects of the current landfill and the proposed expansion.

The information that proponents and their consultants dispense to the lay public can be incomprehensible and overwhelming. Experts can evaluate the proponent's data and advise what is valid and what they regard as propaganda or spin. They can also interpret data and assess the significance of findings. The best approach is to have the environmental lawyer select the experts they would like to work with. This leads to a team that can work comfortably together with the lawyer and citizens.

Any group involved in such a fight needs to be clear on the reasons for opposing the project in their community. In the case of the Richmond Landfill, citizens needed to understand why the landfill should not be expanded at that site. Steve Medd, a local resident and geologist, volunteered to educate the group about the physical characteristics of the site. In time, almost everyone in the community knew about fractured limestone, the thin glacial till overlying the limestone plain, and why the geology of the site made it unsuitable for garbage disposal. Residents learned that leachate was produced by the action of rain and snowmelt on garbage piled on soil. They also learned about the high potential for leachate to contaminate wells and local streams, and the health effects of exposure to contaminated water and air. They used this knowledge when it came time to write letters to the ministry. And write they did, again and again.

The dump opponents set up a storefront office in Napanee—to dispense project information and collect signatures. Citizens opposed to the dump expansion walked the streets and shopping malls, went to church services, and knocked on doors. They went to wherever there were people. These efforts generated a record number of letters to the Ministry of the Environment for an environmental assessment. Was it worth it? The dump opponents believed it affected the outcome—Minister Laurel Broten alluded to the public response in her letter outlining her rejection of the dump expansion. At his first meeting with citizens in a Marysville parish hall in 1999, Rick Lindgren had said, "We want a paper trail at the end of the day." And a paper trail formed—petitions, postcards, and letters. More than eight thousand letters washed up on the ministry's shores. There was no question that the unprecedented number of submissions to the ministry sent a clear collective *no* from the community.

I asked Rick why he had worked so hard and so long for this particular citizens' group, especially since he was always in great demand elsewhere. His answer: "I liked the work and I also liked the people and enjoyed working with them." Several dump opponents explained what kept them engaged year after year on such a contentious and exhausting project. Jeff Whan said he had mastered some basics of geology and hydrogeology, and whatever else he needed to know about landfills, but now he couldn't get out because he was carrying in his head the history of the landfill fight. Moreover, Ian Munro, Marilyn Kendall, Steve Medd, and other activists have become some of his best friends. Ian Munro, who assumed the chair of CCCTE in December 2015, reiterated that friendships kept him committed. "You couldn't let people down," he said. How, then, do you keep people engaged in an environmental fight for the long haul? Get them working together on a common cause, especially one with ethical implications. Bonds and loyalties are bound to develop, and the rest will follow.

Another important aspect of the dump fight was informing and lobbying local and provincial politicians, ministry bureaucrats and policy advisers, the environment minister, the environmental commissioner, and so on. Key members of the landfill opposition group targeted bureaucrats, especially those directly involved in the Richmond Landfill file. Chief Don Maracle, for his part, lobbied local and provincial politicians, ministry officials, and environment ministers, sometimes threatening civil unrest if the dump expansion were to be approved. The successful fight against the Richmond Landfill can be attributed to a dedicated lawyer, a dedicated team, and a dedicated First Nation chief. The landfill opponents caution that anyone wishing to embark on a dump fight should be prepared to have it consume their lives, and be prepared to spend enormous amounts of time and energy on fundraising.

The alliance between the Mohawk community and the white population—the two groups had lived as two solitudes for centuries—was a critical development. The close relationships forged were apparent at the tribunal victory celebration, where the Mohawks shared their cultural practices with their neighbours. The Mohawks have always had to worry about safe drinking water, and they got involved in the dump fight out of concern for their well water—it was already contaminated, and they didn't want it further polluted by landfill leachate. People outside the reserve are protecting their well water too—six domestic wells near the landfill have already been contaminated. No one at the outset thought that this common thread would come to bind the two groups. The local white residents now understood more fully the situation of many Indigenous groups, who have had long-standing problems accessing safe drinking water. The Mohawks also wielded considerable political power. Dump opponents readily acknowledged that success would not have been possible without their Mohawk allies.

Margaret Walsh realized decades ago that political office increased her ability to influence decisions. She was councillor and then reeve of Tyendinaga Township—by the time she retired in 2010, she was in her late eighties. Steve Medd and Ian Munro were having trouble convincing Greater Napanee town council to stop staying neutral or supporting the landfill company. Taking a page out of Margaret's playbook, they decided that they would be more effective if they were members of council—better, they surmised, to be on the inside than on the outside. Both ran for council seats in the municipal elections of 2014, but didn't get in. This did not deter Ian. The election bid had given him a higher profile, and he continued to lobby town council. It paid off when council did an about face and unanimously passed a resolution in the spring of 2016 declaring Greater Napanee an "unwilling host" for a mega-landfill. Mission accomplished.

At the same time, Mike Bossio cast for bigger fish; he applied to run for the federal Liberal party in the fall 2015 federal election. Unopposed for the nomination, he became the Liberal candidate for Hastings–Lennox and Addington. Mike soon put a campaign team together and started knocking on doors. Who was on his team? Friends he had made in the dump fight, of course, among them Jeff Whan and Ian Munro. Mike won the election by a slim margin; he was pushed over the edge by his alliance with the Mohawk community, who turned out to vote for the Liberal candidate. He took his experience in the dump fight—and his concern for drinking water—to Ottawa as a member of Parliament.

***

Canada produces more garbage per capita than most other advanced industrial nations. In a 2007 report by the Conference Board of Canada, we rank last out of 17 countries.[65] In 2008 statistics, each Canadian generates some 777 kilograms of municipal waste annually, more than twice as much as the best-performing country, Japan, which produces about 377 kilograms per capita.[66] Japanese manufacturers, not consumers, are responsible for the costs of processing and disposing packaging. Here in Canada, the mess is left to consumers. (As an aside, I marvelled on a recent trip to Japan at the cleanliness of the streets and public spaces. No garbage, no pieces of paper anywhere, and no garbage cans in sight. I was quickly advised to take my garbage home.)

We Canadians tend not to recycle much of the garbage we produce, but instead send it to landfills. In Canada, the waste diversion rate is about 30 per cent, which means that an average of 67 per cent is dumped at landfills (less than 5 per cent is incinerated).[67]

How many landfills are there in Canada? According to Landfill Inventory Management Ontario, at least 2,400 landfills are scattered across the country.[68] In Ontario, there are 882 operating landfills—32 large landfills and 850 small ones.[69] Ottawa, with four large garbage dumps within its boundaries and an additional proposed landfill pending approval, has been called the dump capital of Canada.[70]

At one time, landfills were small local dumps operated by municipalities or private parties to serve local communities. These small dumps are fast disappearing—the Ontario Ministry of the Environment and Climate Change currently lists 1,525 small dumps closed.[71] This decrease is driven in part by more stringent government regulation to protect human health and environment, a shift that has fostered a growing need for long-haul garbage transportation services. Garbage is now typically transported long distances to regional facilities or mega-landfills owned and managed by major waste management corporations. For example, Toronto shipped its garbage to Michigan from 2003 to 2010. At its height, 142 trucks a day were making the trip, hauling thousands of tonnes of garbage daily.[72] This practice is one that contributes to global warming. In 2014, emissions from transportation were the largest contributor to Canada's greenhouse gas emissions, representing 23 per cent of overall greenhouse gases. [73]

Some countries have abandoned landfills because of concerns about health and environmental impacts from landfill gas and leachate contamination. Moreover, landfills generate methane, a greenhouse gas that is twenty-one times more potent than carbon dioxide in global warming potential. Emissions from Canadian landfills account for 20 per cent of national methane emissions.[74] Many European countries have instituted landfill bans in recent years, leading to rapid expansion of incineration and development of waste-to-energy technology.

There aren't going to be landfill bans in Canada in the foreseeable future—although there's a hint of that possibility in Ontario's *Waste-Free Ontario Act, 2016*—or a shift to incineration, as the incineration facilities we have are mostly old and polluting. The country has plenty of land available for landfill sites, but not all locations are suitable. It is therefore crucial that those proposing to open new landfills carry out a site selection process to ensure that the land chosen is safe and appropriate for waste disposal. Not uncommonly, as in the case of the Richmond Landfill, a landfill development is piggybacked onto an existing landfill that may have been located in an unsuitable site in the first place.

***

I have been asked many times why I undertook to write this book. Rick Lindgren has been encouraging. "There are numerous brawls about dumps, landfills, incinerators, and other waste disposal facilities (including radioactive waste sites) all over Ontario," he told me, "and these garbage wars are not likely to stop soon. . . . While I'm involved in many of these other fights, I can't do them all—some concerned citizens will be acting on their own and will need a good primer on how to wage war against risk-laden disposal proposals."

Ian Munro recalled the first approval of the dump expansion in the 1980s, by an Ontario government clearly aware of the potential problems. "That decision will leave a massive and dangerous legacy," he told me. "I don't want that repeated. Also, I am fairly sure that once this abomination is fully killed, other communities will know it can be done. Ideally, the Ministry of the Environment and Climate Change will get the message and stop facilitating this nonsense, but failing that, concerned citizens will have a blueprint to guide their efforts and, hopefully, boost their optimism that success is possible." This is my hope—that the book will serve as a guide to citizens fighting dump wars and other unwanted developments.

Now that we have arrived at the end of this story—though the Richmond Landfill saga itself is not over—what can I say that I have learned? I've learned that farmers, who led the opposition in the beginning, have an emotional attachment to their land and are willing to commit and sacrifice a great deal to protect their little piece of earth. They recruited their immediate neighbours and the nearby Mohawk community, and then they attracted some smart, highly educated and trained people, who took the ball and ran with it. They also recruited me and we learned to fight as hard as they did to protect what the late Allan Gardiner called his paradise. I have been involved in this battle for the past decade and have been recording deeds and misdeeds for most of that time. I've learned never to underestimate ordinary country folk, as they call themselves—they are capable of extraordinary achievements.

EPILOGUE

On July 8, 2013, three parties—Concerned Citizens Committee of Tyendinaga and Environs, Canadian Environmental Law Association, and the Mohawks of the Bay of Quinte—sent an application to Ontario's environmental commissioner requesting changes to provincial legislation governing landfills. They submitted an Application for Review under the *Environmental Bill of Rights*, which allows citizens to request review and amendment of an existing Act in order to protect the environment. The application requested that the ministry review and revise section 27 of the *Environmental Protection Act*, which regulates the establishment, expansion, and operation of waste disposal sites.[75]

There had been precedents for revisions to section 27. In Ontario, no party is allowed to establish, operate, or expand a landfill unless approval has been obtained under the *Environmental Protection Act*. This general prohibition had occasionally been strengthened by the Ontario legislature through amendments to the EPA that prohibit landfills in particularly sensitive areas. In 1994, for example, the legislature amended the EPA to prohibit new or expanded landfills within the Niagara Escarpment Plan Area due to concern about adverse ecological impacts. Similarly, that same year, in response to public opposition to the Adams Mine Landfill proposal, the legislature enacted statutory changes that prohibited landfilling in natural or artificial lakes greater than one hectare.[76]

In view of overwhelming evidence against placing waste disposal sites on fractured bedrock, the application requested that the Ministry of the Environment review and revise section 27 to prohibit new and expanded waste disposal sites at hydrogeologically vulnerable locations across the province. The applicants further submitted a "no means no" amendment to section 27, to prohibit repeated applications for a previously rejected waste disposal site in an unsuitable location. This was particularly called for in the Richmond Landfill case, where Waste Management was proposing a new adjacent landfill on fractured bedrock at the same time that it was attempting to develop acceptable contingency measures for a closed landfill leaking leachate off-site.

"Over the decades," said Rick Lindgren, "CELA has represented concerned citizens across the province in a number of cases involving proposed landfills at inherently unsuitable fractured bedrock locations. It is time for Ontario to catch up with other jurisdictions in Canada and the U.S., which preclude siting landfills on fractured bedrock."[77]

Mike Bossio reiterated that if CCCTE's suggested changes were adopted, it would mean their fight with Waste Management would finally be over. "It really behooves the MOE to step forward and finally settle this issue about where to locate dumps, for everybody's sake. I certainly don't want to see another community go through what we've gone through for 15 years. It's not right, it's not fair, to impose that kind of burden."[78]

The environmental commissioner, who was responsible for reviewing and reporting on the government's compliance with the *Environmental Bill of Rights*, forwarded a copy of the Application for Review to the Ministry of the Environment, which administers the *Environmental Protection Act*.

In a short letter dated October 2, 2013, the ministry advised the applicants that it would not undertake their requested review of the Act. "The current site specific assessment process allows for the ministry to have sufficient understanding of the risks and suitability of the associated mitigation measures, to determine whether a particular site is suitable for the landfill proposed," wrote Anne Neary of the Ministry of the Environment. "Therefore the ministry has concluded that a prohibition of landfill siting in statute is not required." However, she indicated that the ministry would "conduct a review of guidance materials related to the ministry's landfill approval processes, to determine if changes could be made to further enhance the level of protection to human health and the environment."[79]

In a blog posted on CELA's website, Lindgren expressed his frustration. "Aside from this brief commentary defending the status quo, the MOE refusal letter was essentially unresponsive to the legal and technical issues described in the EBR application." He said that the offer for review was unacceptable because the guidance materials were "non-binding and generally unenforceable in law," and did not "address the current gap in section 27 of the EPA." He reiterated that CELA would continue to push for these changes to the Act "in order to establish clear legislative rules on which types of sites are off-limits to landfilling for hydrogeological reasons."[80]

The applicants were convinced that they were not going to hear from the ministry again on this issue. And that was the end of that.

Three years later, there was a surprising turn of events—a phone call from the environmental commissioner's office in the spring of 2016 about setting up a meeting to hear an update from the ministry on the request for review. Then silence. The proposed meeting never materialized. Perhaps ministry officials were not ready for a presentation.

In another surprising turn of events, Ian Munro received a phone call in September 2016 from Steve Klose, director of Environmental Sciences and Standards Division of the Ministry of the Environment and Climate Change. Klose advised that he and his staff were working on the commitment made when the ministry rejected the 2013 *Environmental Bill of Rights* section 27 Application for Review. He confirmed that the ministry was completing an internal review and had hired a consultant to also review the landfill approval processes in other jurisdictions. He wanted to know if CCCTE was interested in participating in the process. Ian Munro informed him that CCCTE definitely had a position on the issue. Klose assured Munro that CCCTE would be provided with the reports when they were completed. Ian wondered whether the environmental commissioner's interest in the matter had something to do with this sudden development.

Two days later, Ian heard from Heather Brodie-Brown, the ministry's senior contaminant hydrogeologist. She advised that the ministry was conducting a review of guidance materials to make improvements that will provide clear requirements for site characterization and to minimize the number of applications submitted that may be rejected due to site concerns. The Ministry of the Environment and Climate Change hopes to consult with the applicants and will make their reports available prior to consultation meetings. Ian says the words seem reasonable at face value, but obviously the devil will be in the details.

More information came from Dianne Saxe, Ontario's environmental commissioner. When anti-dump advocates read the 2015/2016 Environmental Protection Report released in October 2016, they learned that the review included "two parts: a scan looking at best practices in leading jurisdictions (anticipated to be completed June 2016); and a review of the state of the science regarding site conditions and performance of selected existing Ontario landfills (anticipated to be completed in September 2016). The ministry anticipated that the review would be completed by October 2017."[81] The applicants thought this was better late than never. What next? Now they are waiting to hear from the ministry—and perhaps the environmental commissioner. They take some comfort in knowing that the environmental commissioner of Ontario is keeping on top of the Richmond Landfill file.

While they were waiting, they had an interesting diversion. Auditor General Bonnie Lysyk tabled her 2016 Annual Report in the Legislative

Assembly of Ontario on November 30, 2016.[82] It was a very bad day for the Ministry of the Environment and Climate Change. In a scathing rebuke of the ministry, the report contained strongly worded criticisms of Ontario's environmental approvals and environmental assessment programs. A number of issues raised in the report were familiar to the citizens involved in the Richmond Landfill fight. In fact, they had first-hand knowledge of aspects of these programs, in part, because of their participation in the flawed Richmond Landfill environmental assessment process. And then they had to file an *Environmental Bill of Rights* application for leave to appeal problematic conditions in an Amended Environmental Compliance Approval the ministry issued for the landfill, culminating in the hearing of the Environmental Review Tribunal.

Richmond dump opponents paid particular attention to the auditor general's comment that public complaints were not well managed. They certainly had knowledge about those. Did the residents not lodge hundreds, and perhaps thousands, of complaints with the ministry about odour emissions from the landfill, which elicited no response? They have frequently asserted that they have to carry out functions, such as oversight of compliance, that are rightfully those of the ministry. Thus, the issues highlighted by the auditor general's 2016 report resonated with these citizens, and they applaud her report.

Back to the Ministry of the Environment and Climate Change. The dump activists were still waiting, as they have done endlessly over the years. Even if the reports came, they would not represent what Ian Munro referred to as an obvious "end of the story." He reiterated, "We know how these things go and these reports will no doubt be a 'starting point' for more consultation leading to an unsatisfactory conclusion that, ultimately, will probably require some community like ours to challenge the MOECC once again in some legal or quasi-legal forum to get a genuine change in policy—and you know . . . how long all that will take."

And indeed, in March 2017, two reports from the ministry came in: *State of the Science Review of Landfill Siting and Site Characterization and Risk in Relation to Landfills* and *Landfill Siting Jurisdictional Review*. After reviewing the documents, Richmond dump activists believed no major policy changes regarding the siting of landfills would be forthcoming. However, the Ministry of the Environment and Climate Change advised Ian Munro by phone that it was planning to develop policy and procedural changes, and would be ready for discussions sometime in the summer. Following the conversation, Munro concluded that the ministry was not ready to resolve the flaws in landfill siting. He advised his fellow activists to prepare their responses to the reports' findings and to also prepare to expect "overwhelmingly disappointing recommendations." The citizen activists, as we have seen throughout this saga, have every intention of following through to ensure the Richmond site is monitored effectively and remains closed forever. And so as the tale of this dump fight comes to an end, the story remains unresolved.

APPENDICES

A. Abbreviations

BREC   Beechwood Road Environmental
        Centre
CARE   Citizens Against the Richmond
        Expansion
CCCTE   Concerned Citizens Committee
        of Tyendinaga and Environs
CELA   Canadian Environmental
        Law Association
EA   environmental assessment
EBR   *Environmental Bill of Rights*
        (Ontario)
ECO   environmental commissioner
        of Ontario
EPA   *Environmental Protection Act*
        (Ontario)
ERT   Environmental Review Tribunal
MBQ   Mohawks of the Bay of Quinte
MOE   Ministry of the Environment
        (Ontario)
MOECC   Ministry of the Environment and
        Climate Change (Ontario)
WMC   Waste Management of Canada
        Corporation

B. Glossary

Alvar. Habitat on a limestone plain with thin or no soil and sparse grassland vegetation. Prone to flooding in the spring and drought in the summer, it supports a group of rare plants, birds, and animals commonly found on prairie grasslands. Trees and shrubs are absent or severely stunted. The Great Lakes region south of the Canadian Shield is one of three areas in the world where alvars are found.

Contaminant Attenuation Zone. Zone outside the landfill area, established to allow contaminants to naturally deteriorate to levels compatible with the reasonable use of the adjacent properties.

Contingency plan. A course of action or activities designed by an organization to respond effectively when unexpected events or setbacks occur.

Drumlin. An oval-shaped mound of glacial till with a height as great as 40 metres and a length ranging from 100 to 5,000 metres. One end is blunt and the other is sloped gently and points to the direction of glacial advance. Drumlins rarely occur singly and tend to occur in groups. Lennox and Addington County has about 175 drumlins strewn across its southern end that provide good agricultural land on a limestone plain.

Environmental Advisory Committee. Committee formed at the time of the Richmond Landfill expansion project that consisted of community members and officials from the municipalities of Greater Napanee and Tyendinaga Township and the Mohawks of the Bay of Quinte. The objective was to facilitate discussion between committee members and the landfill company and its consultants regarding the terms of reference.

Environmental assessment (EA). A process governed by the *Environmental Assessment Act* that sets out a decision-making process so that the potential impacts are considered before a project begins. Public consultation is mandatory.

Environmental Assessment Board. Formed in 1975, it held hearings about waste or sewage disposal sites as well as environmental assessments. It was merged with the Environmental Appeal Board and its role was taken over by the Environmental Review Tribunal.

Environmental Bill of Rights (EBR). Passed by the Ontario legislature in 1993, it gives Ontario citizens rights to participate in environmental decision-making. Upheld by the environmental commissioner.

Environmental Compliance Approval. A government document for unique types of operations, such as landfills, that sets out the conditions of operation that must be met.

Environmental commissioner of Ontario (ECO). An independent officer of the legislature; the province's environmental watchdog.

Environmental Review Tribunal (ERT). An independent, quasi-judicial body. Its primary role is adjudicating applications and appeals under various environmental and planning statues.

Fractured limestone. Limestone bedrock with fractures that are mostly horizontal but also vertical.

Glacial till. Sediment consisting of a mixture of rocks, sand, and clay deposited directly from glacial ice.

Hydrogeology. The area of geology that deals with the distribution and flow of groundwater in soil and rock.

Landfill gas. Composed of many different gases created by the action of microorganisms within a waste mound, landfill gas contains 40 to 60 per cent methane; the remainder is mainly carbon dioxide, with trace amounts of volatile organic compounds.

Landfill leachate. Solutions of liquids from waste or from rainwater or snowmelt that contain waste constituents such as organic contaminants and ammonia.

Landfill liner. A barrier that is laid down under an engineered landfill site, generally made up of a layer of compacted clay and a high-density polyethylene geomembrane. It is intended to retard the migration of leachate and its toxic constituents into underlying aquifers or nearby water bodies. Landfill liners are believed to ultimately fail.

Leachate collection system. A drainage system that collects and transports leachate formed within a landfill to a collection sump where it is removed for treatment or disposal.

Leachate plume. When leachate gets into groundwater, the flow rates become slower and the flow paths may be more tortuous. As a result, contaminants tend not to disperse but to form slugs.

Limestone plain. Flatland consisting of a limestone base overlain with a thin layer of soil. Limestone pavement, a horizontal surface of exposed limestone produced by weathering, is often found on the limestone plain. Due to weathering action along cracks and crevices, the surface appears to be broken up into regular segments like artificial pavement.

Napanee Plain. Flatland that consists mostly of a limestone base covered with a few centimetres of soil. The plain is an area of approximately 1,800 square kilometres that spreads from Napanee to Kingston to the east and Belleville to the west, south to Lake Ontario and north to the southern portion of Stone Mills.

Overburden. Natural rock and soil in the top layer of the earth.

Public Liaison Committee. Struck when Laidlaw Waste Systems Ltd. took over the Richmond Landfill, the committee's mandate was to oversee the activities of the landfill. It was made up of landfill officials, municipal representatives, an MOE official, and community members.

Reasonable use. Guideline B-7 is used as a basis for determining the reasonable use of groundwater on properties adjacent to sources of contaminants such as a disposable site, and for determining the levels of contaminants that may be discharged off-site. For drinking water, the water quality may not be degraded in excess of 25 per cent of the Ontario Drinking Water Objective for a health-related parameter, which is a standard set by MOECC for the quality of safe drinking water.

Terms of reference. Prepared by the proponent, a document that provides the scope and work-plan of a proposed project. It must be submitted to the provincial Ministry of the Environment and Climate Change for approval. The environmental assessment must adhere to the approved terms of reference.

C. Chronology of Events

1954
Fred Sutcliffe starts collecting garbage in Richmond Township

1971
Sutcliffe receives Certificate of Approval for Sutcliffe Sanitation Services Ltd. (15,000 tonnes/year on 9.0 acres)

September 1985
Sutcliffe submits application to the Ministry of the Environment (MOE) for expansion of dumpsite (125,000 tonnes /year on 40 acres)

January 1986
Hearing of Environmental Assessment Board on Sutcliffe's expansion application; recommends approval

August 1987
Ministry issues Provisional Certificate of Approval No. A371203 to Sutcliffe Sanitation Services Ltd. for waste from all Ontario municipalities

December 1987
Tricil Ltd. purchases Sutcliffe Sanitation

February 1988
Residents form first opposition dump committee: Richmond/Tyendinaga Environmental Association

February 16, 1988
First major dump meeting: 200 residents, Sutcliffe family, officials from Tricil Ltd. and MOE

January 1990
Laidlaw Waste Systems (Ottawa) Ltd. purchases Richmond Landfill from Tricil Ltd.

March 1997
Laidlaw Waste Systems (Ottawa) Ltd. changes name to Canadian Waste Services (Ottawa) Ltd.

August 1997
Canadian Waste Services (Ottawa) Ltd. changes name to Canadian Waste Services Inc.

December 1997
Public consultation meetings begin for the Public Liaison Committee on terms of reference

January 1998
Amalgamation of Ontario municipalities— Napanee, Richmond, North Fredericksburgh, South Fredericksburgh, and Adolphustown amalgamated into Town of Greater Napanee

March 1998
Media release announcing Richmond Landfill expansion project (750,000 tonnes/year on 237 acres)

February 8, 1999
Margaret Walsh organizes dump meeting, Mohawks attend, Andrew Maracle collapses and dies; formation of Stop the Richmond Dump Expansion Citizens Committee

June 17, 1999
Last public consultation meeting (joint Public Liaison Committee and Environmental Advisory Committee) for terms of reference

June 1999
Canadian Waste Services Inc. submits terms of reference of environmental assessment for landfill expansion

July 1999
Concerned Citizens Committee of Tyendinaga and Environs (CCCTE) retains environmental lawyer Richard Lindgren of Canadian Environmental Law Association

September 1999
Minister of the environment approves terms of reference

June 26, 2000
CCCTE incorporated

September 2000
CCCTE submits application to Divisional Court for judicial review of minister's approval of terms of reference

June 2003
Divisional Court quashes minister's decision to approve terms of reference

July 2003
Canadian Waste Services Inc. files motion for leave to appeal to Ontario Court of Appeal

April/May 2004
Canadian Waste Services Inc. changes name to Waste Management of Canada Corporation (WMC)

August 2004
Ontario Court of Appeal strikes down decision of Divisional Court

November 2004
WMC resumes environmental assessment

March 2005
Supreme Court of Canada denies leave to appeal minister's approval of terms of reference

November 2005
WMC submits environmental assessment; public comment period begins

January 2006
Public comment period ends

June 2006
Ministry of the Environment releases government review—recommends non-approval of environmental assessment

November 2006
Minister announces decision to reject WMC's proposed expansion

June 2007
WMC submits closure plan to MOE

October 2008
CCCTE, MBQ, and Township of Tyendinaga submit application under the *Environmental Bill of Rights* requesting permanent closure of the Richmond Landfill site

December 2008
MOE denies request for closure of Xthe Richmond Landfill site

October 2009
Ontario environmental commissioner presents annual report at Queen's Park—calls for closure of Richmond Landfill

June 2010
WMC submits terms of reference for new landfill expansion (Beechwood Road Environmental Centre) to MOE

June 2011
Closure of Richmond Landfill site

January 2012
Director, MOE, issues Amended Environmental Compliance Approval (formerly Certificate of Approval) No. A371203

January 2012
CCCTE submits application under the *Environmental Bill of Rights* for leave to appeal Amended Environmental Compliance Approval No. A371203

February 2012
Minister approves terms of reference for Beechwood Road Environmental Centre

March 2012
Environmental Review Tribunal (ERT) grants leave to appeal seven conditions in Amended Environmental Compliance Approval No. A371203

June 25, 2012
Preliminary ERT hearing: Mohawks of the Bay of Quinte (MBQ) and Napanee Green Lights granted intervenor status

July 8, 2013
CCCTE, CELA, and MBQ submit application under the *Environmental Bill of Rights* requesting review and amendment of section 27 of the *Environmental Protection Act* (EPA)

October 2, 2013
MOE denies request for review and amendment of section 27 of the EPA

April 13, 2015
ERT hearing begins in Belleville

June 22, 2015
Final arguments; ERT hearing ends

July 21, 2015
ERT issues interim order—more testing and more frequent monitoring; 1,4-dioxane reporting level: 1.0 ug/L. Completion of further work and testing by WMC by September 30, 2015. WMC requests two extensions to December 1, 2015.

December 2015
CCCTE Christmas potluck dinner and
meeting; Ian Munro elected chair of
CCCTE to replace Mike Bossio (MP in
Ottawa), Marilyn Kendall elected secretary
December 24, 2015
ERT issues Order for Case No. 12-033:
CCCTE v. Ontario (Environment and
Climate Change)
April 2016
Town of Greater Napanee council passes a
resolution requesting WMC to withdraw the
BREC proposal and the MOECC to stop
the impending environmental assessment
July 27, 2016
District manager advises WMC that
delineation of leachate plume not
completed. New deadline for submission
of Contaminant Attenuation Zone delinea-
tion report: December 30, 2016. Due
dates extended to February 15, 2017,
then to May 31, 2017, and recently to
July 15, 2017.

D.   Cast of Characters

Beatty, Brian: Engineering consultant
for Sutcliffe Sanitation Services at Environmental Assessment Board hearing in
1986; later, consultant for Tricil Ltd.

Bechard, Kevin: Divisional vice-president
for facility development for Canadian
Waste Services and later Waste Management of Canada.

Berger, Thomas: Judge from British
Columbia who headed the 1970s Royal
Commission for the Mackenzie Valley
Pipeline.

Bishop, John: Area manager (Eastern
Region), Ministry of the Environment;
represented the ministry at Environmental
Assessment Board hearing in 1986.

Blair, Mary: Resident on Selby Road
north of Richmond Landfill; complained
of rats.

Bossio, Mike: Chair of CCCTE and
long-time opponent of Richmond Landfill
expansion; in 2015 elected Liberal member of Parliament for Hastings-Lennox and
Addington. Married to Irene, daughter
Hailey and son Lucius.

Bradley, James: Ontario minister of the
environment (1985–1990) in the Liberal
government of David Peterson; (2011–2013)
in the Liberal government of Dalton
McGuinty; (2013–2014) in the Liberal
government of Kathleen Wynne.

Brant, Joseph (Thayendanegea): Mohawk
leader who led a large group of Six
Nations to a site on the Grand River in
Ontario.

Brodie-Brown, Heather: Senior contaminant hydrogeologist, Ontario Ministry of the Environment and Climate Change.

Broten, Laurel: Ontario minister of the environment (2005–2007) in the Liberal government of Dalton McGuinty; rejected environmental assessment for proposed expansion of the Richmond Landfill in 2006.

Burns, Barry: Surface water engineer; represented Ministry of the Environment at Environmental Assessment Board hearing in 1986.

Butts, Carolyn: Artist in Tamworth, Ontario, and active member of CCCTE.

Calver, Bud: Mayor of the Town of Greater Napanee (1997–2001).

Carter-Whitney, Maureen: Chair of Environmental Review Tribunal hearing held from April 13 to June 22, 2015; released her ruling on December 24, 2015.

Chadwick, Rob: Member of the Chadwick family, who are early residents in the area; bought farmland from Ben Sutcliffe.

Clement, Tony: A member of the Ontario Progressive Conservative government (1995–2003), and minister of the environment (1999–2000); now a federal member of Parliament.

Cranston, Doug: Doug and his wife, Betty, raised purebred cattle on a farm next to the Sutcliffe farm on Callaghan Road.

Dahme, Harry: Counsel for Waste Management of Canada Corporation.

Daly family: Immigrants from Ireland in 1800s; founded Daly Tea Company in Napanee area.

DePoe, Eric: Paralegal; owner of Waterfall Tearoom in Yarker and member of CCCTE; married to Barbara Linds.

Deserontyon, Captain John: In 1784, led Mohawk families from Lachine to the Bay of Quinte to territory granted by the Simcoe Deed/Treaty 3 ½; group later called the Mohawks of the Bay of Quinte.

Dombrowsky, Leona: Member of the Legislative Assembly of Ontario, representing Hastings-Frontenac-Lennox and Addington; Ontario minister of the environment (2003–2005), minister of agriculture, food and rural affairs (2005–2010) in the Liberal government of Dalton McGuinty.

Dourson, Michael: Expert witness (toxicologist) for Waste Management at ERT hearing.

DuChene, Seth: Editor, *Napanee Beaver*; married to Mary Beth; son Calvin and daughter Ryan.

Elliott, Brenda: Ontario minister of the environment and energy in the Progressive Government of Mike Harris (1995–1996); responsible for not renewing the *Intervenor Funding Project Act.*

File, Ed: Retired York University professor, dump opponent, and early member of CCCTE.

Finkle, Paul: Resident of Tyendinaga Township and dump opponent.

Ford, Franklin: Engineering consultant for Sutcliffe Sanitation Services Ltd. at Environmental Assessment Board hearing in 1986.

Fox, Gary: Member of Legislative Assembly of Ontario (1995–1999), representing Prince Edward-Lennox-South Hastings for the Progressive Conservative Party.

Gardiner, Allan: Farmer and resident of Richmond Township; initiated opposition to Richmond Landfill expansion; chair of Richmond/Tyendinaga Environmental Association; chair of Public Liaison Committee. His wife, Iris, and son Iain were both supportive of Allan's involvement in the dump fight.

Geneja, Steve: First chair of CCCTE; responsible for obtaining legal aid and acquiring Richard Lindgren as counsel.

Gerretsen, John: Member of the Legislative Assembly of Ontario, representing Kingston and the Islands for the Liberal Party (1995–2014); Ontario minister of the environment (2007–2010); attorney general (2011–2014).

Gillespie, Eric: Counsel for Mohawks of the Bay of Quinte.

Hardeman, Ernie: Member of the Legislative Assembly of Ontario, representing Oxford County for the Progressive Conservative Party.

Harper, Stephen: Conservative prime minister of Canada (2006–2015).

Harris, Mike: Progressive Conservative premier of Ontario (1995–2002), elected on the platform of the Common Sense Revolution.

Hartin, Gary: Reeve of Richmond Township. Supported proposed dump expansion of Sutcliffe Sanitation; regrets this decision on his retirement.

Hick, Wellington: Last person buried in the pioneer cemetery (Empey Hill Cemetery) in 1906.

Hill, Earl: Chief of Mohawks of the Bay of Quinte (1968–1973, 1980–1993); did not receive notification of Environmental Assessment hearing in 1986.

Hineman, Kelley: Warden of Lennox and Addington (1996).

Holland, Cyril: Surface water evaluator; represented Ministry of the Environment at Environmental Assessment Board hearing in 1986.

Homenuck, Peter: IER Planning, Research and Management Services; public consultation facilitator for Canadian Waste Services.

House, Harlan: Internationally renowned ceramic artist and painter, resides in Lonsdale, dump opponent and supporter of CCCTE, donated his artworks to raise funds for the dump fight.

Jackson, Winnifred: Elderly resident of Richmond Township, lived near Richmond Landfill.

Johnson, Peter: Resident of Richmond Township and member of Richmond/Tyendinaga Environmental Association.

Kendall, Marilyn: Local writer and member of CARE and CCCTE; wrote "Discourse on the Dump" column for the *Napanee Beaver*; involved in communications and lobbying of bureaucrats and local politicians. Married to Ian Munro.

Kennelly, Steve: Active dump opponent.

Kimmerly, Grant: Resident of Richmond Township, attended meeting of local citizens to form Richmond/Tyendinaga Environmental Association.

Kimmerly, Helen: Attended meeting of local citizens to form Richmond/Tyendinaga Environmental Association. Applicant for Judicial Review of Terms of Reference for Richmond Landfill expansion.

Klose, Steve: Director of Environmental Sciences and Standards Division, Ontario Ministry of the Environment and Climate Change.

Lavigne, Avril: Local resident, recorded with Steve Medd before becoming pop star.

Lindgren, Richard (Rick): environmental lawyer, staff of Canadian Environmental Law Association; counsel for CCCTE since 1999; wife Laura Lee, daughters Anna and Rachel.

Linds, Barbara: Married to Eric DePoe; active volunteer in local theatre activities.

Lysyk, Bonnie: Auditor General of Ontario (2013–).

Maracle, Andrew: Mohawk Elder known as the storyteller. Attended first dump opposition meeting, gave an inspiring talk, collapsed and died at meeting.

Maracle, Betty: Mohawk resident with knowledge of Mohawk traditions.

Maracle, David: Mohawk musician.

Maracle, R. Don: Chief of the Mohawks of the Bay of Quinte (1993–); dedicated and vocal opponent of Richmond Landfill expansion and operations.

Maracle, Kimberly: Mohawk resident with knowledge of Mohawk traditions.

McBain, Bruce: Resident of Marysville; dump opponent; owner of Watermark Books in Lonsdale.

McCulloch, Paul: Counsel for the director, Ontario Ministry of the Environment.

McGuinty, Dalton: Liberal premier of Ontario (2003–2013).

McKnight, Ethel: Resident of Richmond Township, complained of vermin.

Medd, Steve: Geologist and musician; active member of CARE and CCCTE; married to Kathy, daughters Stefanie and Carolyn.

Miller, Gord: Environmental commissioner of Ontario (2000–2015); called for closure of the Richmond Landfill.

Miron, Ian: Counsel for Napanee Green Lights.

Moore, Shayla: Schoolgirl who wrote to Minister Laurel Broten about the dump.

Morley, Andrew: Official of Ontario Ministry of the Environment.

Mowbray, William MacDonald: Sold plot of 90 acres on Lot 1, Concession IV, to Fred Sutcliffe Sr.

Mowers, John: Local farmer who sold Fred Sutcliffe Sr. a plot of 50 acres in Lot 3, Concession IV, and a plot of 20 acres in Lot 3, Concession III. Died in 1978. Had three daughters, Beatrice, Irene, and Geraldine. Irene, now in her nineties, is the only surviving daughter.

Muldoon, Paul: Former executive director of CELA and current member of the Environmental Review Tribunal of Ontario.

Munro, Ian: Member of CARE and CCCTE, media relations, communications, and research; lobbying of bureaucrats and local politicians; liaison between CCCTE and Greater Napanee town council, elected chair of CCCTE in 2015. Married to Marilyn Kendall.

Murphy, Kevin: Local farmer.

Neary, Anne: Assistant deputy minister, Environmental Sciences and Standards Division, Ontario Ministry of the Environment.

O'Connor, Howard: Active member of CCCTE, Second World War veteran; continued flying an airplane for recreation. Died in 2013.

O'Mara, James: Director of the Environmental Assessment and Approvals Branch, Ontario Ministry of the Environment, when Minister Laurel Broten rejected the environmental assessment for the proposed expansion of the Richmond Landfill.

Parsons, Ernie: Member of the Legislative Assembly of Ontario, representing Prince Edward-Hastings (1999–2007) for the Liberal party, and supporter of CCCTE.

Rae, Trish: Historical researcher for the Mohawks of the Bay of Quinte.

Rankin, Walter: Local postman who operated a municipal dumpsite on his property beside the Napanee River; sold contract for a municipal dumpsite and a truck to Fred Sutcliffe Sr.

Reddom, George: Spokesperson for Tricil Ltd.

Remington, David: Mayor of the Town of Greater Napanee (2001–2003).

Richard, Sylvio: Regional manager of Richmond Landfill under Tricil Ltd.

Ruland, Wilf: Hydrogeologist retained by CCCTE.

Ryan, Don: Chair of CARE; played a major role in the fight against Richmond Landfill expansion.

Sammon, Mary Lynne: Active member of CCCTE, responsible for communications for CCCTE; married to Patrick Sammon; died in 2015.

Saxe, Dianne: Environmental commissioner of Ontario, appointed in 2015.

Schermerhorn, Gord: Mayor of Town of Greater Napanee (2003–).

Schindler, Patrick: Counsel for the Mohawks of the Bay of Quinte.

Schliesmann, Paul: Editorial writer at *Kingston Whig-Standard*.

Scott, Heather: Developed the CCCTE website LeakyLand.com.

Scott, Ian G.: Counsel for the 1970s Royal Commission on the Mackenzie Valley Pipeline; attorney general of Ontario (1985–1990) under the Liberal government of David Peterson; instituted the *Intervenor Funding Project Act* in 1990 that was repealed in 1996 by Mike Harris's Progressive Conservative government.

Scott, Robert: Lawyer in Belleville; represented Richmond/Tyendinaga Environmental Association and local citizens in first meeting with Tricil Ltd. and Ministry of the Environment.

Seanor, Art: Project engineer for Waste Management of Canada.

Shelley, Don: Resident of Richmond Township. He and his wife, Christine, met with other local citizens to form Richmond/Tyendinaga Environmental Association.

Shelley, Rick: Resident of Richmond Township, livestock farmer, and early member of CCCTE; married to Linda, daughter Kimberlee.

Shelley, Tim: Attended a meeting of local citizens to form Richmond/Tyendinaga Environmental Association.

Shipley, Kevin: Engineer with XCG Consultants Ltd., and consultant for Mohawks of the Bay of Quinte.

Silver, Christine: Collected newspaper clippings on dump issues for the use of CCCTE.

Stafford, Don: Resident of Tyendinaga Township and member of Richmond/Tyendinaga Environmental Association.

Stephenson, Kyle: Hydrogeologist at the Ontario Ministry of the Environment in Kingston; identified leachate plume migrating outside boundaries of Richmond Landfill property.

Stewart, Jack: Resident of Tyendinaga Township and member of Richmond/Tyendinaga Environmental Association.

Stewart, Penny: Official of Ontario Ministry of the Environment.

Sutcliffe, Ben: Resides adjacent to Richmond Landfill; nephew of Fred Sutcliffe Sr. Ben and his wife, Janet, are members of CCCTE; applicant for Judicial Review of Terms of Reference for the proposed Richmond Landfill expansion. Breeds horses and dogs.

Sutcliffe, Fred, Sr.: Established dumpsite and garbage collecting operation (Sutcliffe Sanitation Services Ltd.) in Richmond Township; wife Mary, two sons (Fred Jr. and Ben) and three daughters (Mary, Sylvia, and Eileen); family sold their garbage business to Tricil Ltd. in December 1987.

ter Braak, John and Lillian: Sold home and farm of 200 acres on Lot 2, Concession IV, to Fred Sutcliffe Sr. for $10,000.

Thompson, Bernice: Resident of Selby; member of CCCTE; caretaker of Tweedsmuir papers.

Touzel, Tom: Physician in Greater Napanee; heads environmental group called Napanee Green Lights.

Tucker, Gary: Resident of Tyendinaga Township and member of Richmond/Tyendinaga Environmental Association.

Tulloch, Janelle: Active member of CCCTE; spearheaded restoration of Empey Hill Cemetery; maintains CCCTE's flower fund. Married to Ken Tulloch.

Tulloch, William and Margaret: Ancestors of Ken Tulloch buried in 1865 in the pioneer cemetery (Empey Hill Cemetery).

Varette, Jack: Site manager of Richmond Landfill under Canadian Waste Services.

Vittal, Priya: Assistant to lawyer Eric Gillespie.

Walsh, Margaret: Organized first dump meeting; united Mohawks and CCCTE members; schoolteacher; reeve of Tyendinaga Township (1998–2010); councillor (2010–2014). Son John Walsh sold house in Lonsdale to Mike Bossio.

Walters, Michael: Division landfill manager, Canadian Waste Services.

Weaver, William: Councillor for Ward 3 (South Fredericksburgh) (1998–2000).

Whan, Jeff: Retired IBM executive; active member of CCCTE; maintains CCCTE website LeakyLand.com; married to Janet.

Witmer, Elizabeth: Ontario minister of the environment (2001–2002) in the Progressive Conservative government of Mike Harris.

Winter, Bert: First farmer to sell farmland to Laidlaw Waste Systems (parts of three lots in Concession IV and two lots in Concession III for a total of 264.5 acres).

Young, Basil: Married to Sylvia Sutcliffe, daughter of Fred Sutcliffe Sr.

Young, Duane: Grandson of Fred Sutcliffe Sr. and son of Basil and Sylvia Young; died in an accident in 1964.

NOTES

1. The environmental assessment for a project is governed by the provincial *Environmental Assessment Act*. The first environmental assessment law in Canada was passed in July 1975 by the Province of Ontario and pro- claimed in force in October 1976. Although the Act initially applied to public sector undertakings including projects and plans of provincial and municipal agencies (unless exempted), it could also be applied on a case-by- case basis to certain private sector undertakings that were designated by regulation. The Richmond Landfill expansion was designated by regula- tion to be governed by the Act. The terms of reference set out the propo- nent's work plan for the proposed project. If approved, the environmental assessment must adhere to the terms of reference.

2. Marilyn Kendall, "Fair Play Forgotten in EA Process," *Napanee Beaver,* April 14, 2006.

3. Annual Income Statement for Waste Management Inc., www.marketwatch.com.

4. Seth DuChene, "Mega-dump Plans Unveiled: Richmond Landfill Site Subject of Major Expansion Applica- tion," *Napanee Beaver,* March 11, 1998.

5. Report of the Environmental Assess- ment Board (EP-85–02), Feb. 20, 1986.

6. Paulette Peirol, "Deseronto Garbage Firm Sold to Tricil," *Kingston Whig-Standard,* Jan. 19, 1988.

7. Report of the Environmental Assess- ment Board (EP-85–02), Feb. 20, 1986; Provisional Certificate of Approval for a Waste Disposal Site, Provisional Certificate of Approval A371203, issued to Tricil Limited, 89 Queensway West, Suite 800, Missis- sauga ON L5B 2V2.

8. Paulette Peirol, "Tricil Garbage Dump Waste Volume Upsets Residents," *Kingston Whig-Standard,* Feb. 6, 1988.

9. Paulette Peirol, "Napanee Commercial Waste Pickup Rates Some Companies Won't Sign with Tricil after Rates Rise as Much as 200%," *Kingston Whig-Standard,* Feb. 3, 1988.

10. No one I talked to could remember the date of the meeting; I found it in Chris Malette, "Richmond Residents Outraged at Tricil's Landfill Site," *Belleville Intelligencer,* Feb. 17, 1988.

11. Agency of Toxic Substances and Disease Registry, U.S. Department of Health and Human Services, Public Health Service, Toxicological Profiles: Phenol.

12. E.L. Baker et al., "Phenol Poisoning due to Contaminated Drinking Water," *Archives of Environmental and Occu- pational Health* 33 (1978), 89–94.

13. Stephen Ecker, "Residents Pack Empty Hill Church to Fight Land Fill Site," *Loyalist Country Living*, March 1988.

14. Paulette Peirol, "The Reeve Never Sleeps on Monday: Workaholic Gary Hartin Says Goodbye to Richmond Township Turmoil," *Kingston Whig-Standard*, Nov. 16, 1988.

15. Dominik Wisniewski, "Protesters Erupt at Landfill Meeting," *Napanee Beaver*, Nov. 30, 2005.

16. Ibid.

17. Seth DuChene, "Dump Fight Goes to the Top," *Napanee Beaver*, Sept. 10, 2004.

18. Dominik Wisniewski, "Supreme Court Won't Hear Landfill Appeal," *Napanee Beaver*, March 16, 2005.

19. Dominik Wisniewski, "Dump Foes Update Council," *Napanee Beaver*, July 1, 2005.

20. Thomas R. Berger, "The Mackenzie Valley Pipeline Inquiry (1976–1977)," second annual lecture in honour of Professor J.A. Corry, *Queen's Law Journal* 3,1 (1976), 3–16.

21. Carolyn Swayze, *Hard Choices: A Life of Tom Berger* (Vancouver: Douglas & McIntyre, 1987), 139.

22. EBR Registry No. PA6E1000, "Sun-setting of the Intervenor Funding Project Act," March 28, 1996.

23. M. Mittelstaedt, "Environmental Intervenor Funds Cut Off by Ontario: Conservation Groups Lose Bid to Save Law Financing Challenges to Sensitive Projects," *Globe and Mail*, April 1, 1996.

24. Ibid.

25. Legislative Assembly of Ontario, Debate on Second Reading of "Bill 76, Environmental Assessment and Consultation Act, 1996," *Hansard*, June 24, 1996, at 1800.

26. Lydia Miljan and Zachary Spicer, "Municipal Amalgamation in Ontario," Fraser Institute, 2015.

27. Seth DuChene, "Town Swamped by Dump Findings," *Napanee Beaver*, Oct. 25, 2000.

28. Annette Phillips, "Dump Study Infuriates Residents," *Kingston Whig-Standard*, Jan. 12, 2001.

29. *Napanee Beaver*, Nov. 28, 2013.

30. Seth DuChene, "Expert Raises New Stink on Landfill Plan," *Napanee Beaver*, June 25, 2003.

31. Ibid.

32. Dominik Wisniewski, "WM Gets Earful at Landfill Meeting," *Napanee Beaver*, Dec. 8, 2004.

33. Ibid.

34. For the Simcoe Deed, see *Indian Treaties and Surrenders: From 1680 to 1890* (Ottawa: Brown Chamberlin, Printer to the Queen's Most Excellent Majesty, 1891) [Facsimile edition reprinted, Toronto Cole's 1971], vol. 1, 7–8.

35. Amendment to Environmental Compliance Approval A371203, Notice 10, Jan. 9, 2012, Ministry of the Environment.

36. "Waste, Recycling Drop-offs Resume at BREC Site," *Napanee Beaver*, Jan. 26, 2012.

37. Seth Duchene, "BREC Terms of Reference Approved," *Napanee Beaver*, Feb. 23, 2012.

38. Environmental Commissioner of Ontario, "Richmond Landfill Site: Time for Closure," *Building Resilience, ECO Annual Report, 2008–09* (Toronto: Environmental Commissioner of Ontario, 2009), 103–106.

39. Ibid.

40. Dominik Wisniewski, "Close Landfill Now: ECO," *Napanee Beaver*, Oct. 8, 2009.

41. *Environmental Assessment Act*, R.S.O. 1990, E.18. The Harris government amended the Act when it came into power; the amended Act came into effect in January 1997.

42. "Improving Environmental Assessment in Ontario: A Framework for Reform: A Report Prepared by the Minister's Environmental Assessment Advisory Panel—Executive Group," March 2005.

43. "Dump Opponents Have Duty to Protest," Feb. 2, 2000.

44. Jennifer Pritchett, "Waste Giant Wines and Dines Napanee Leaders," *Kingston Whig-Standard*, June 3, 2005.

45. "A Case of Bad Judgment," June 4, 2005.

46. "Public Opinion against Dump Expansion Overwhelming," opinion commentary (letter), June 1, 2005.

47. Dominik Wisniewski, "Dump Foes Update Council," *Napanee Beaver*, July 1, 2005.

48. Seth DuChene, "MPP Cool to Dump Plans," *Napanee Beaver*, March 3, 1999.

49. Seth DuChene, "Local MPP Plans Postcard Protest," *Napanee Beaver*, Jan. 29, 2000.

50. Charlie Cray, 3rd ed., Dec. 1991, Greenpeace U.S.A. Toxics Campaign.

51. Adam Bramburger, "Expert Outlines Landfill Concerns," *Napanee Beaver,* May 19, 2006.

52. "Review under the Environmental Assessment Act," June 2006, Ministry of the Environment, Environmental Assessment and Approvals Branch, Toronto, Ontario, June 2006.

53. Letter to Kevin Bechard, Director, Public Affairs, Waste Management of Canada Corporation, from Laurel C. Broten, Minister of the Environment, November 3, 2006.

54. Samantha Craggs, "Richmond Expansion Is Dead," *Belleville Intelligencer*, Nov. 4, 2006.

55. Dominik Wisniewski, "Minister Rejects Dump Expansion," *Napanee Beaver*, Nov. 8, 2006.

56. Ibid.

57. Jordan Press and Jennifer Pritchett, "Province Dumps Landfill Plan," *Kingston Whig-Standard*, Nov. 4, 2006.

58. Dale Morrisey, "Richmond Landfill Expansion Denied," *Napanee Guide*, Nov. 10, 2006

59. Seth DuChene, "What's Next for Richmond Landfill Site?" *Napanee Beaver*, Nov. 22, 2006.

60. Beth Primeau, "Dump Foes Mark Big Win," *Napanee Beaver*, Nov. 22, 2006.

61. Ibid.

62. Seth DuChene, "Despite Agreement, Landfill Fight Goes On," *Napanee Beaver*, April 18, 2013.

63. Ministry of the Environment and Climate Change, "Warwick Landfill Expansion: Project Information about This Environmental Assessment," www.ontario.ca, March 20, 2014, updated July 30, 2014.

64. Ministry of the Environment and Climate Change, "West Carleton Environmental Centre: Project Information about This Environmental Assessment," www.ontario.ca, March 20, 2014, updated July 30, 2014.

65. Conference Board of Canada, "How Canada Performs: A Report Card on Canada," June 2007.

66. Conference Board of Canada, "How Canada Performs: Municipal Waste Generation," www.conferenceboard.ca.

67. Statistics Canada, Envirostats: Waste in Canada, www.statcan.gc.ca.

68. Province of Ontario, Ministry of the Environment and Climate Change.

69. Province of Ontario, Large Landfill Sites (from 2011); Small Landfill Sites (from 2010), www.ontario.ca/data.

70. "Ottawa: The Garbage Dump Capital of Canada," NoDump.ca.

71. Province of Ontario, "Small Landfill Sites List," www.ontario.ca/data.

72. "Toronto Garbage No Longer Shipped to Michigan," CBC News, Toronto, www.cbc.ca, Dec. 30, 2010.

73. "Municipal Solid Waste and Greenhouse Gases," Environment and Climate Change Canada, www.ec.gc.ca.

74. "Greenhouse Gas emissions by Economic Sector," ibid.

75. *Environmental Protection Act*, R.S.O. 1990, c. E.19.
27. (1) No person shall use, operate, establish, alter, enlarge or extend a waste management system or a waste disposal site except under and in accordance with an environmental compliance approval. 2010, c. 16, Sched. 7, s. 2 (20).

76. Richard Lindgren, "How to Say 'No' to Unsuitable Landfill Sites in Ontario," blog, Canadian Environmental Law Association, www.cela.ca, Oct. 17, 2013.

77. Seth DuChene, "Groups Seek Law Change," *Napanee Beaver*, July 18, 2013.

78. Ibid.

79. Letter from Anne Neary, Assistant Deputy Minister, Environmental Sciences and Standards Division, Ministry of the Environment, Oct. 2, 2013.

80. Lindgren, "How to Say 'No.'"

81. Environmental Commissioner of Ontario, 2015/2016 Environmental Protection Report: *Small Steps Forward*, Oct. 26, 2016, 58–59.

82. Auditor General of Ontario, *2016 Annual Report, Volume 1: Reports on Value-for-Money Audits* (Introduction). Ministry of the Environment and Climate Change: Environmental Approvals, 298–337; Environmental Assessments, 338–85 (Toronto: Office of the Auditor General of Ontario).

INDEX